Great Careers

Hospitality,
Human
Services,
and Tourism

with a High School Diploma

Titles in the *Great Careers* series

Great Careers

Hospitality, Human Services, and Tourism

with a High School Diploma

Rowan Riley

Ferguson Publishing
An imprint of Infobase Publishing

Great Careers with a High School Diploma
Hospitality, Human Services, and Tourism

Ferguson
An imprint of Infobase Publishing
132 West 31st Street
New York, NY 10001

ISBN-13:978-0-8160-7048-0

Library of Congress Cataloging-in-Publication Data

Great careers with a high school diploma. — 1st ed.
    v. cm.
  Includes bibliographical references and index
  Contents: [1] Food, agriculture, and natural resources — [2] Construction and trades — [3] Communications, the arts, and computers —
[4] Sales, marketing, business, and finance — [5] Personal care services, fitness, and education — [6] Health care, medicine, and science —
[7] Hospitality, human services, and tourism — [8] Public safety, law, and security — [9] Manufacturing and transportation — [10] Armed forces.
  ISBN-13: 978-0-8160-7046-6 (v.1)
  ISBN-10: 0-8160-7046-6 (v.1)
  ISBN-13: 978-0-8160-7043-5 (v.2)
  ISBN-10: 0-8160-7043-1 (v.2)
[etc.]
1. Vocational guidance — United States. 2. Occupations — United States.
3. High school graduates — Employment — United States.
  HF5382.5.U5G677 2007
  331.702'330973 — dc22

                                                              2007029883

Ferguson books are available at special discounts when purchased in bulk quantities for businesses, associations, institutions, or sales promotions. Please call our Special Sales Department in New York at (212) 967-8800 or (800) 322-8755.

You can find Ferguson on the World Wide Web at
http://www.fergpubco.com

Produced by Print Matters, Inc.
Text design by A Good Thing, Inc.
Cover design by Salvatore Luongo

Printed in the United States of America

Sheridan PMI 10 9 8 7 6 5 4 3 2 1

This book is printed on acid-free paper.

Contents

How to Use This Book

This book, part of the Great Careers with a High School Diploma series, highlights in-demand careers that require no more than a high school diploma or the general educational development (GED) credential and offer opportunities for personal growth and professional advancement to motivated readers who are looking for a field that's right for them. The focus throughout is on the fastest-growing jobs with the best potential for advancement in the field. Readers learn about future prospects while discovering jobs they may never have heard of.

Knowledge—of yourself and about a potential career—is a powerful tool in launching yourself professionally. This book tells you how to use it to your advantage, explore job opportunities, and identify a good fit for yourself in the working world.

Each chapter provides the essential information needed to find not just a job but a career that draws on your particular skills and interests. All chapters include the following features:

- ☆ "Is This Job for You?" presents a set of questions for you to answer about yourself to help you learn if you have what it takes to work in a given career.
- ☆ "Let's Talk Money" and "Lets Talk Trends" provide at a glance crucial information about salary ranges and employment prospects.
- ☆ "What You'll Do" provides descriptions of the essentials of each job.
- ☆ "Where You'll Work" relates the details of the settings typical of that field.
- ☆ "Your Typical Day" provides details about what a day on the job involves for each occupation.
- ☆ "The Inside Scoop" presents firsthand information from someone working in the field.
- ☆ "What You Can Do Now" provides advice on getting prepared for your future career.
- ☆ "What Training You'll Need" discusses state requirements, certifications, and courses or other training you may need as you get started on your new career path.
- ☆ "How to Talk Like a Pro" defines a few key terms that give a feel for the occupation.

✯ "How to Find a Job" gives the practical how-tos of landing a position.

✯ "Secrets for Success" and "Reality Check" share inside information on getting ahead.

✯ "Some Other Jobs to Think About" lists similar related careers to consider.

✯ "How You Can Move Up" outlines how people in each occupation turn a job into a career, advancing in responsibility and earnings power.

✯ "Web Sites to Surf" lists Web addresses of trade organizations and other resources providing more information about the career.

In addition to a handy comprehensive index, the back of the book features an appendix providing invaluable information on job hunting strategies and techniques. This section provides general tips on interviewing, constructing a strong résumé, and gathering professional references. Use this book to discover a career that seems right for you—the tools to get you where you want to be are at your fingertips.

Introduction

For millions of Americans, life after high school means confronting the real world and adulthood. It's a world filled with life-altering decisions and daunting questions. While this sort of responsibility is nothing to shrug at, if you're motivated and know what you want out of life, starting a career after high school doesn't have to be a frightening experience. For some, it's even exciting.

Each year, more than 900,000 of the nation's 2.8 million high school graduates go directly into the workforce. While it's often easier to find a job with a degree in hand, the past decade has shown significant growth in the number of jobs that don't require a college diploma. According to the Economic Policy Foundation (EPF), a nonprofit based in Washington, D.C., only 23 percent of the jobs available in the coming years will require a four-year degree or higher.

At this point, you're probably thinking, "Yes, but don't college graduates land all the high-paying jobs?" While it's true higher education can lead to higher earnings in professions involving medicine, science, or the law, in recent years that historic gap between the wages of high school graduates and those with college degrees has begun to close. Between 2000 and 2004, the yearly earnings of college graduates dropped by 5.6 percent while the earnings of high school graduates increased by 1.6 percent (EPF).

The reason for this change in tides is simple: Too many jobseekers now have college degrees, and there aren't enough college-level jobs to accommodate them. Unless you graduate at the top of your class or attend an Ivy League school, finding a job can be a major struggle for college graduates.

College does give certain students the type of confidence, focus, and direction that they wouldn't otherwise find at a desk job. It is an invaluable experience for those who can afford it, but the escalating cost of college can be a major deterrent for many high school students. According to the College Board, the average tuition price of a four-year public college during the 2006–2007 school year was $5,836, and this figure doesn't even take into consideration the cost of housing, books, or transportation.

Spend Your Time and Money Wisely

If you're someone who values hands-on experience more than classroom discussion, college may not be for you, at least for the time being. There are many career paths available for people with high school degrees, and since most of the jobs don't require a huge time or money investment, you can test-drive a career without a major commitment. Instead of investing thousands of dollars into a degree that you don't know what to do with, why not make some money first and get a jump start on your career?

So what career should you consider? The range is so broad that Great Careers with a High School Diploma includes 10 volumes, each based on related career fields from the Department of Labor's career clusters. Each volume profiles about 10 careers, which, if you do the math, means there are almost 100 career options for you to consider.

Every job has different training requirements, which is why Great Careers features jobs that require little or no training beyond high school as well as those that do. In most cases, if the job requires additional training, it can be completed either on the job, through a certificate program, or during an apprenticeship, which combines entry-level work and class time. Regardless of your education or experience level, Great Careers is designed to get you through the often nail-biting process of applying for a job. For example, each chapter has a section on getting hired, which provides job hunting tips specific to each career. And for high school students looking to jump-start their careers, there's a section called "What You Can Do Now," which gives advice on how to get ahead through volunteer work, internships, academic classes, and extracurricular activities.

Having more than 100 careers to choose from can be a bit overwhelming, which is why each chapter offers a self-assessment quiz that helps answer the question, "Is this job for me?" What's more, each chapter provides insight into what you'll do, who you'll work for, where you'll work, and how much you're likely to earn.

In this volume of Great Careers, you will be introduced to an exciting array of careers in the hospitality industry. Many of the jobs featured in this volume offer flexible hours and part-time work, but what really sets this volume—and indeed this industry—apart from the rest are the unique and diverse places where you can find work. Anywhere people go for leisure, there are jobs to be had at hotels, restaurants, and bars—not to mention at baseball stadiums.

All hospitality jobs share a common purpose: to service people in the best way. Every job is designed to make people's lives a bit brighter, whether it's by preparing an exquisite meal, making sure someone's flight is enjoyable, or putting together a beautiful bouquet of flowers. It's a fun and fast-paced industry filled with jobs that affect

people's lives in a positive way, so if you enjoy working in crowded environments, and have a friendly or outgoing disposition, this may be the field for you.

There's Room for You in Hospitality

If you are new to the hospitality industry or you've never worked before, one of the easiest places to land a job is the food and beverage industry. Not only is it the nation's largest employer outside of the government, but it's also known for hiring young and inexperienced workers. According to the National Restaurant Association, 27 percent of adults got their first job experience in a restaurant. So if you enjoy cooking and can handle fast-paced environments, the first job profiled in this volume may really get your interest.

Cooks and food-prep workers spend a lot of time on their feet and often have to cook or prepare more than a hundred meals per day. The work can be stressful and demanding, but if you can handle the pressure of sautéing onions, chopping vegetables, and cooking salmon all at the same time, then you might really enjoy working in a kitchen for a living.

On the other hand, if you love the atmosphere of restaurants, but your idea of cooking is popping a frozen entrée into the microwave, then you should consider working in what is called the front end of the restaurant. Chapter 2 profiles the responsibilities of waiters, waitresses, hosts, and hostesses. The work can be just as stressful, but instead of searing scallops and lifting large pots of boiling water, waiters and hosts make sure that the customers are satisfied and everything is running smoothly.

In order to work in the front end, you must be fast on your feet and friendly. If this sounds interesting, you should also check out Chapter 3, which profiles bartenders. Although some bartenders work in the front end of restaurants, they're more frequently found in late-night establishments, such as bars, clubs, and lounges. This job requires more training than that of a waiter or even food-prep worker because not only do you need to know how to mix hundreds of drinks, but you also have to be skilled at dealing with disturbances caused by drunken patrons.

If the food service industry sounds too fast-paced for your liking, then the hospitality jobs featured in Chapters 4 and 5 might be more your speed. Floral arrangers and dry cleaning workers typically work in small, quiet environments. Though their clientele can be just as demanding, both floral arrangers and dry cleaners create their own deadlines and work at a pace that is comfortable for them. If you're at all artistically inclined, you might really enjoy the art of picking flowers and arranging bouquets and displays. With customers who may return every week, successful dry cleaners are organized and personable.

One of the greatest aspects of the hospitality industry is that there are plenty of opportunities to run your own business. Many careers profiled in the chapters of this book can lead to management or ownership positions if you stick it out and work hard. At many hospitality jobs, the managers value experience as much as—if not more than—a college education. The industry is built on ambition and hard work, which is part of the reason why it attracts so many entrepreneurs and go-getters. It is not uncommon to hear of young people taking the money that they would have spent on college and investing it in their own restaurant, bar, bed-and-breakfast, or florist shop.

If you're interested in opening your own business, keep in mind that it requires more than just "people skills." You must be sharp, good with numbers, and have excellent leadership and management skills. These skills can be hard to develop without any guidance, which is why this book gives you advice on how to sharpen your business acumen through classes, seminars, internships, certifications, and part-time work. Although some of the jobs call for more formal training, every job in this volume essentially requires the same thing: hard work and gumption.

If travel interests you, then you should definitely read the profile on flight attendants in Chapter 6. This is one of the more exciting and cosmopolitan jobs featured in this volume. You get to travel and meet new people, and it's hard to beat the benefits—free flights to wherever you want and an excellent health and retirement program. That said, the actual job is not as easy as most smiling flight attendants make it look. The hours are long, you're away from home a lot, and the safety of every passenger is in your hands. In addition, the application and training process is intense, so if you're really considering the job, be sure to carefully read the section "What Training You'll Need."

If you would prefer a job that's closer to home and doesn't require as much training, you might want to read Chapter 7, which profiles desk clerks, concierges, and reservation agents. Like flight attendants, these three jobs require you to deal with a revolving door of international customers, many of whom have been traveling all day and are tired or irritable. Their satisfaction and safety is one of your primary responsibilities.

However, unlike flight attendants, these three positions require little or no experience and training. More important, employers in these fields often hire high school students on a part-time basis. So even if these jobs are not the perfect fit for you, working as a desk clerk, concierge, or reservation agent is a great stepping-stone to other jobs in and outside of the hospitality industry.

If it's high stakes, suspense, and spontaneity that you're after, then take a look at Chapter 8, which presents the work of professional umpires. More so than the other jobs in this volume, this profession carries a tremendous amount of on-the-spot pressure. The integrity of every baseball game rests on the umpire's shoulders. The job is so critical to the sport that several umpires have even been admitted into the Baseball Hall of Fame. But before you start dreaming of your own baseball card, the road to the major leagues is long and only a select few make it. If you're not deterred by the extensive training requirements after reading Chapter 8, pick up a Major League Baseball rule book and start studying.

Lock In Your Spot

So now you know a little of what awaits you in the job features in this volume of Great Careers. There are many faces to the hospitality industry; perhaps one of the careers of this volume will interest you, or perhaps they will point you in a fresh direction. One thing is certain: Whenever money is paid, money is received. There might be room for you in the hospitality trade. If you have special skills, play them to your advantage. If you have years of experience canoe tripping, you may have a considerable edge as a guide for an ecotourism country. Start exploring your options now.

Unlike other industries, hospitality employers aren't looking for good grades and fancy degrees. What they value most is employability skills: commitment, responsibility, a willingness to learn, flexibility, and above all, enthusiasm. Some careers require more initial training than others, but with hard work every job in this volume—and others in the rich universe of hospitality, human services, and tourism that we have not sampled here—is obtainable. And if you stick with it, they can lead you to a satisfying and lucrative career.

Work in a dynamic environment

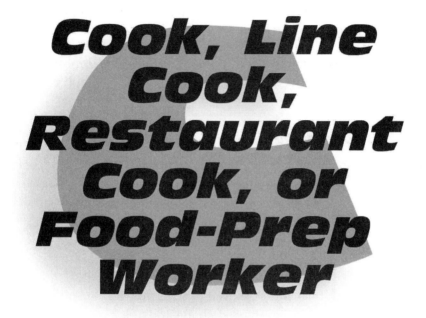

Cook, Line Cook, Restaurant Cook, or Food-Prep Worker

Bask in the glory of a satisfied customer's smile

Create new and exciting dishes

Cook, Line Cook, Restaurant Cook, or Food-Prep Worker

A generation ago, dining out was reserved for dates and special occasions; nowadays it's a way of life. The rise in two-income households and the number of busy, overcommitted adults has created a boom in the restaurant industry. Americans now spend 48 percent of their food budget in restaurants, which is one reason the restaurant industry is a great place to work. Of course, being a chef is by no means as easy as Rachel Ray or the Food Network makes it look. The hours are long, the work is physically demanding, and the atmosphere can be high pressure, but the thrill of watching your smiling customers savoring one of your meals makes it worth the while.

Is This Job for You?

Answer the following questions to see whether a career as in cooking or food prep is right for you.

Yes	No	**1.**	Can you handle a fast-paced environment?
Yes	No	**2.**	Do you have a love of food?
Yes	No	**3.**	Do you enjoy cooking for others?
Yes	No	**4.**	Are you safety-minded and responsible?
Yes	No	**5.**	Do you work well in stressful situations?
Yes	No	**6.**	Are you in good shape and able to lift heavy pots and pans?
Yes	No	**7.**	Do you have strong teamwork skills?
Yes	No	**8.**	Can you be on your feet for hours?
Yes	No	**9.**	Are you interested in cooking techniques and principles?
Yes	No	**10.**	Do you have a sharp sense of taste and smell?

If you answered "Yes" to most or all of these questions, you should consider a career as a cook. To find out more about this job, read on.

What You'll Do

A cook's job varies, depending on the position in the kitchen and the type of dining establishment. This said, all cooks are responsible for creating and preparing exciting dishes under tight time pressures. If

Let's Talk Money

The median hourly earnings for a restaurant cook is $9.39, but this amount can vary depending on the type and location of the establishment and specific job duties. For example, a cafeteria cook typically earns $10.38 an hour, whereas a prep worker's median hourly earning is $8.04, according to the Bureau of Labor Statistics.

you are working in a large restaurant, you and your fellow kitchen workers may have to prepare dozens of meals in three hours. To accomplish such an overwhelming undertaking, you must be physically fit and able to work well with others. Cooking in a professional kitchen is practically a sport, and if one player is down, the rest of the team suffers. While landing a job an executive chef position at an upscale restaurant requires extensive training, there are plenty of kitchen jobs available to those with little or no training. Here is a brief introduction to some of the kitchen players:

- Food preparation workers are in charge of prepping the food. They chop the vegetables, trim the meats, stir the sauces, and keep the work areas clean.
- Assistant cooks (sometimes referred to as line cooks) manage a specific station. Their title usually indicates what they cook. For example, the fry cook manages the frying station.
- Short-order cooks work in establishments that emphasize quick service, such as coffee shops, diners, or lunch counters. They handle multiple orders at the same time and are the ones grilling burgers, frying eggs, and cooking french fries simultaneously.

Who You'll Work For

- Full-service restaurants
- Coffee shops and diners
- Cafeterias in hospitals, schools, and corporations
- Limited dining establishments in park and recreation centers
- Resort, hotel, and casino dining establishments, which may offer seasonal employment
- Catering companies and banquet halls, which may also operate on a seasonal or part-time basis

Let's Talk Trends

The restaurant industry currently employs an estimated 12.8 million people, making it the nation's largest employer outside of the government. What's more, the industry is expected to add 2 million more jobs over the next decade.

Where You'll Work

Insiders say one of the perks of being a cook is that you can find employment in any state. Though well-paid jobs are largely confined to the big cities, destination towns, and high-end resort areas, today there are thousands of restaurants in every state and at least one in every town. In other words, expertise as a cook is great to have if you like to travel and want to be mobile.

The shift you take—morning, afternoon, or evening—will greatly affect your duties. If you work in a coffee shop or a local restaurant that attracts the lunch crowd, the morning and afternoon shifts are typically the most chaotic. Everyone wants to eat quickly at get back to work, so orders will be flying at you right and left. Although the morning and afternoon shifts are often the most chaotic kitchen environment, the good news is that your day is usually over by 4 p.m. or 5 p.m. On the contrary, upscale restaurants or restaurants with large bars usually attract the dinner crowd. Cooks on the evening shift usually work until midnight or later, and as a result, they are usually paid more money.

Working nights at a popular restaurant can be extremely trying. The hours are long and the dishes are more elaborate to prepare; however, if you want to climb the culinary ladder, working the night shift will put more money in your pocket and demonstrate that you are a hard worker.

Your Typical Day

Here are the highlights of a typical day in the kitchen of a small restaurant.

✓ **Get started.** When you first walk in, you turn on the ovens. If everything looks in order, you head to the refrigerator and examine

The Inside Scoop: Q&A

Milton Pinkney
Head cook
Los Angeles, California

Q: *How did you get your job?*

A: My aunt had a restaurant, and as a kid in Louisiana, I always liked to hang out in it. When I moved to Los Angeles, I started working as an assistant cook at the Cozy Corner in downtown L.A. Once the head cook left, I took over for him. That restaurant eventually closed, so I came here as head cook. When I first started, we just had counter seating, but over the years we've expanded to become a 65-seat restaurant.

Q: *What do you like best about your job?*

A: Seeing a smile on a customer's face when they get up from one of our meals. I also like to create new dishes, but mostly I like making our customers happy. It's very flattering when someone from as far away as New York passes by fancier restaurants to come to our café. We put out quality food, and I'm proud of that.

Q: *What's the most challenging part of your job?*

A: The hours. I get up almost every day at 4 in the morning to bake the pies, roast the turkeys, and prepare the soups and sauces. We cook all of our meals on the premises and all of our ingredients are fresh, so it takes a lot of time and effort.

Q: *What are the keys to success to being a cook?*

A: Being consistent. If your quality of food is consistent, in time you will develop a loyal following. I try to treat every customer like a family member. Restaurants thrive on word of mouth, so if you make a mistake, you're probably losing more than just one customer.

your food supply. Let's say you have a lot of cabbage left over from the day before, you'll probably want to add a cabbage soup to "Today's Specials."

✔ **Begin prep.** After the menu and today's specials have been decided, it's time to start preparing the foods. This is largely the prep workers' job, but everyone lends a hand. Vegetables are sliced, soups and sauces are made ahead of time, and meats are thawed and prepared for cooking.

✔ **Get into high gear.** Once customers start arriving, the kitchen kicks into high gear. You are simultaneously grilling burgers, poaching eggs, and, perhaps, filleting salmon. Depending on where you work and how busy it is, you may have to prepare 50 or more orders in a few hours. Time becomes a blur. Then once your shift starts to wind down, you're almost wiped out.

What You Can Do Now

✦ Look for a vocational-education course or program in culinary careers at your high school.

✦ Try to find a part-time job or internship at a local restaurant or coffee shop.

✦ Learn about and experiment with food. Cooking is supposed to be fun, so try to cook as much as possible for your family, friends, and coworkers.

✦ Check out cooking techniques. For instance, check out the how-to videos on epicurious.com.

What Training You'll Need

Above all else, what you'll need to succeed in the culinary world is a strong work ethic coupled with a lot of on-the-job experience. Paying your dues, so to speak, is an integral part of becoming a good chef. Many of the celebrity chefs that you see on television initially began as short-order cooks or prep-workers. Emeril Lagasse started as a baker in a small Portuguese bakery in Massachusetts, and today he has six restaurants and five cookbooks to his name. While a fancy culinary degree can get your foot in the door, If you demonstrate leadership skills and an eagerness to learn new cooking techniques, you might move up fast in the culinary world.

If you have the time, summer internships or part-time jobs are both great ways to break into culinary field. Even if you have zero experience in the kitchen, chances are good that you can find work as a food-prep worker. The job requires little training, and you'll be able to see first-hand how a kitchen is run. For high school students, vocational schools usually offer culinary courses that prepare students for work as a short-order cook at a diner or a cook's assistant at a fancy restaurant. Most courses begin with kitchen sanitation and go on to teach basic training in preparing food, such as slicing and dicing methods for meats and vegetables, as well as basic cooking methods, such as baking, broiling, and grilling. Although internships and cooking classes will help you land a job, don't underestimate the training that can be found in your own kitchen. If you experiment with food and cook as much as possible for your family, friends, and coworkers, you'll eventually develop your own cooking style—something that is hard to accomplish when you are working at a restaurant or in the middle of an instructed class.

How to Talk Like a Pro

Here are a few words you'll hear in a commercial kitchen:

- ✴ **Blanche** To plunge into boiling liquid and cook to 10 to 20 percent of doneness.
- ✴ **Choice grade** The second-highest USDA quality grade for meat, indicating good-brittle fat, good marbling, and good-textured flesh; the most commonly used grade of meat.
- ✴ **Cost control** The practice of ensuring that food costs are managed so that they stay within a set ranged and so the business can earn a profit.
- ✴ **Slack time** Kitchen jargon referring to time allowed for a product to undergo a change—a frozen product to thaw, juices in cooked meats to settle, dough to rest in baking.
- ✴ **Sous-chef** This French word means, literally, "under-chef." Sous-chefs are skilled cooks working in large or upscale restaurants who work underneath the executive chef. They often supervise the various cooking stations.
- ✴ **Partial cooking** Any cooking process that is stopped before the product is fully cooked, and then refrigerated until needed, at which point it is fully-cooked. This process is often used for large-quantity or commercial cooking.

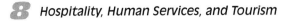

How to Find a Job

The restaurant industry is the largest employer in the U.S. outside of the government, so those working in the restaurant business are not likely to go hungry any time soon. There are dozens of culinary-related jobs listed online or in your local newspaper. For those working in a major metropolis, Craigslist.org can be a great resource. It's not hard to find a job in this field; however, if you are looking to work in an upscale dining establishment, you'll probably need to network a bit.

If you don't know anyone in the restaurant industry, you can always join an association, such as the National Restaurant Association (NRA). For a small membership fee, Associations such as the NRA can put you in touch with top chefs in your area. Persistence is the key to finding a job in the restaurant industry. Because restaurants have such a high turnover rate, jobs go fast. When you see a position that you like, act quickly. A hard worker is the most valuable asset to have in the kitchen, so if you don't have the experience necessary, be sure to stress that you are diligent and dependable person.

Secrets for Success

See the following suggestions and turn to the appendix for advice on résumés and interviews.

- Culinary passion and the ability to work well with others are the two most essential ingredients to becoming a good chef. That said, it is equally important to be an organized and dependable worker.
- Be clean and look clean. Foodborne illness is commonly spread by poor hygiene, especially the failure to wash hands. For this reason most establishments will want to avoid even the appearance of uncleanliness and will want every worker to reflect a regard for good practices.
- Learning Spanish is a good idea. A lot of kitchen staff, especially in cities, speak it as a first language.

Reality Check

The top culinary schools can be as pricey as private colleges, but the wages of chefs and cooks in many parts of the U.S. aren't on par. Figure out the cooking salaries in your area if you're tempted to take out a hefty loan for culinary school, so you know whether you can pay it back.

Some Other Jobs to Think About

✯ Caterer. If you are a social person, who likes cooking but doesn't want to be in the kitchen all day, you might want to consider the catering field.

✯ Maitre d' or hostess. For those who like the atmosphere and vibe of a restaurant, but don't want to get their hands dirty, consider this often well-paid alternative.

✯ Nutritionist. This is a great job for people who live a healthy lifestyle and think that food is the most essential ingredient to a long and happy life.

How You Can Move Up

✯ Put in the extra effort. The restaurant industry doesn't operate on a normal 9-to-5 basis. Putting in long hours and offering to take on more responsibility in the kitchen will go a long way.

✯ Become an expert in a specific culinary field. Specializing in a certain cuisine or type of food, such as desserts or Asian cuisine, can really set you apart from the rest of the group.

✯ Focus on management. Volunteer to help out with administrative tasks such as food ordering and staffing, to help yourself become more valuable.

Web Sites to Surf

The National Restaurant Association. This is the leading business association for the restaurant industry. Their web site offers up-to-date industry facts as well as information on where to find jobs.   http://www.restaurant.org

Star Chefs. A magazine for culinary experts as well as those interested in learning about the culinary industry. It's also a great place to find a job or post your résumé.   http://www.starchefs.com

Create your own working hours

Waiter, Waitress, Host, or Hostess

Work with a diverse group of people

Put a smile on a customer's face

Waiter, Waitress, Host, or Hostess

Like it or not, your waiter, waitress, host, and hostess are just as important to your dining experience as the meal itself. They are the ambassadors of the kitchen. If something is wrong with your meal, it's not the chef you complain to, it's your food servers. A good food server—waitress or waiter—makes customers feel like they are the only ones in the room. He or she is attentive, but not intrusive. During busy hours, when there are 30 tables of customers waiting for food, food servers must be able to multitask with smiles on their faces. In addition to memorizing specials, taking customer's orders, and ringing up a check, food servers must also keep their cool, even when they have a rude patron and seven other tables to serve. Similarly, hosts or hostesses greet and seat customers while tracking what the waitstaff is doing and keep waiting customers happy. If you're friendly, fast on your feet, and good at multitasking, you might consider becoming one of the millions of food servers and host or hostess in the United States.

Is This Job For You?

Would being a waiter, waitress, host, or hostess be right for you? To find out, read each of the following statements and answer "Yes" or "No."

Yes	No	**1.**	Are you a friendly and patient?
Yes	No	**2.**	Do you like helping others?
Yes	No	**3.**	Can you keep your cool in stressful situations?
Yes	No	**4.**	Can you work on your feet for long periods?
Yes	No	**5.**	Are you good at basic arithmetic?
Yes	No	**6.**	Can you anticipate others' needs?
Yes	No	**7.**	Can you keep a professional manner?
Yes	No	**8.**	Would you be willing to work weekends and holidays?
Yes	No	**9.**	Do you like the hustle and bustle of restaurants?
Yes	No	**10.**	Do you have a good memory for specials and orders?

If you answered "Yes" to most of these questions, consider a career as a waiter, waitress, host, or hostess. To find out more about these positions, read on.

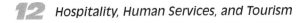

Let's Talk Money

The median hourly earnings (including tips) of waiters and waitresses is $6.75, whereas hosts and hostesses tend to average more at $7.52 an hour, according to 2006 data from the U.S. Bureau of Labor Statistics.

What You'll Do

As a waiter or waitress, your primary responsibility would be to take orders, serve food and beverages, and ensure that the check is accurate and arrives in a timely manner. While these may seem like simple tasks, a shocking amount of sweat and savvy goes into creating a pleasant dining experience. Not only are waiters and waitresses on their feet all day long, they typically carry heavy trays of food-laden dishes. They also must be able to work efficiently. Waiters and waitresses face heavy pressure to serve customers quickly, especially during busy dining periods. Waitresses or waiters who get behind in their orders or mix their orders up can quickly come under fire from belligerent diners. Waitresses and waiters must charm the customer in an unobtrusive way, making sure all of the customer's needs are met, and when something goes wrong in the kitchen—an order is dropped or the steak is overdone—it is the waiter or waitress who must placate the customer and deal with the fallout.

A host's or hostess' primary responsibility is to seat customers in a courteous manner, handing them menus, and escorting them to their tables. Another important part of the job involves caring for the waitstaff and making sure that they are working efficiently. In addition to all this, hosts and hostesses also have to answer the phones, and in most cases, book reservations. If you work in a busy restaurant, this can be the most difficult part of the job. On a busy night, you'll be running around to seat customers, check on the waitstaff to see how the tables are moving, and deal with a menu question or seating problem. Also, depending on the restaurant, you'll have to reserve tables for the following week amidst all the restaurant chaos.

Who You'll Work For

✴ Full-service restaurants

✴ Hotels, resorts, casinos, and cruise ships

✴ Amusement parks and certain other recreational facilities
✴ Corporate cafeterias
✴ Coffee shops and diners
✴ Banquet halls
✴ Assisted living facilities

Where You'll Work

Unlike hosts or hostesses, who typically work at upscale restaurants, a job waiting tables can vary greatly depending on the size and type of establishment. In coffee shops, where straightforward dishes are prepared, fast and efficient service is the most important aspect of the job. In top restaurants where the meals are prepared to order, the emphasis is on customer care. It's important to remember that at a good restaurant the customer is paying for more than just a tasty meal: They're also paying for high-quality service. Waiters and waitresses need to be able to recommend certain dishes and identify ingredients, or explain how various items on the menu are prepared. In some places, a waiter may even be called on to light a flambé at the table.

The shift a waitress or waiter works—morning, afternoon, or evening—will also affect the job environment. Morning and afternoon shifts at local restaurants and coffee shops tend to be the busiest because they typically serve work crowds, most of whom want to eat quickly and without much fanfare. It's an exhausting shift, but the upside is getting all evening off to recover. By contrast, the evening shift tends to be the most stressful at upscale or popular restaurants. Diners are paying more for their meals, and in turn, they expect better service. Although you may initially be less interested in working a busy or stressful shift, keep in mind that you'll make substantially more money in tips during the busy hours.

Let's Talk Trends

These days, dining out is a national pastime. This adds up to more than 2.5 million waiting jobs in the United States, and 328,000 hosting jobs, and research predict steady growth in the demand for hosts, hostess, waiters, and waitresses, in part as boomers start to retire and have more time to eat out.

Your Typical Day

Here are the highlights of a typical evening shift at a restaurant.

✓ **Set up before dinner.** Arrive at 4 p.m. and check in with the host or hostess. If there is a birthday party or special event that evening, you'll probably need to coordinate with the host and help with set-up.

✓ **Serve the meals.** You speed from table to table, taking orders, serving food and drinks, and making sure that the food is prepared well and the customers are satisfied.

✓ **Deliver the check!** Once coffee and deserts have been offered or ordered, it's time to compute the check. It's your job to make sure that everything ordered is accounted for, and that customers receive their checks in a timely manner. Once your last customer's check is closed out, and you've talked with the host or hostess, you've finished your shift.

What You Can Do Now

✯ If you can't find part-time or seasonal work as waiting tables, you might want to try a catering company in your area. The summer and holiday season are the busiest times of year for catering companies, so caterers are always looking for high school or college students to fill in during these times.

✯ Do some research on dining establishments in your area, and decide what sort of restaurant or establishment interests you most.

✯ Have lunch or dinner at the dining establishments that interest you and introduce yourself to the manager or owner.

What Training You'll Need

One of the best parts about being a waiter or waitress is that there is always an abundance of positions at your disposal, and most of them require little or no formal training. At high-end restaurants, previous restaurant experience is often a prerequisite, but for the most part, the training you'll need can be acquired on the job. Although previous restaurant experience gives you a major edge, the most important point to finding work as a waiter or waitress is to project a personable and professional vibe. Good waiters or waitresses are often good

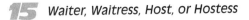

The Inside Scoop: Q&A

Helen Johannesen
Hostess
Madison, Wisconsin

Q: *How did you get your job?*

A: My timing was perfect, though I didn't know it at the time. I just waltzed through the door of L'Etoile restaurant with a thoughtful cover letter and my résumé. You have to take a chance. I believe I got the job because I was motivated, interested, and insisted on hand-delivering my résumé to the maître d'. That way I could have an impromptu interview and really sell myself. I told him that I would work hard and that I had immense respect for the restaurant, and eventually he offered me the job.

Q: *What do you like best about your job?*

A: I like manning the ship. The host stands at the helm of the restaurant and is responsible for getting everyone moving. I like thinking on my feet, solving problems as they arise, interacting with different people, and anticipating the needs of both the patrons and the team around me.

Q: *What's the most challenging part of the job?*

A: Difficult people can be quite challenging. The skill lies in a host's ability to exercise patience, be sympathetic, and diffuse escalating situations that can arise when patrons have to wait for a table or are discontented with the service. Of course the secret to being really good at this job is to think ahead. That way you avoid the possibility of angry or dissatisfied patrons.

Q: *What are the keys to success to being a host or hostess?*

A: Be real. No one wants to contend with a phony hostess who speaks in circles. It's always better to be straightforward with patrons because they can usually tell if you're lying. It's also important to show respect to the kitchen, the servers, the bartenders, and the dishwashers. Finally, you need to take initiative in every aspect of the job. Make yourself an asset to the team.

salespeople. Convincing the customer to order that expensive wine at the beginning of the meal and have that desert and coffee at the end makes employers happy and brings in bigger tips, so previous sales experience or experience working with customers in other positions can be a major plus.

Landing a job as a host or hostess is often more challenging and generally requires previous kitchen or waiting experience. However there are plenty of service industry jobs that will prepare you for the many logistical challenges that hosts and hostesses must deal with on a daily basis. For instance, hotel, resort, or casino jobs, such as front desk manager positions, provide comparable training.

How to Talk Like A Pro

Here are a few words you'll hear as a waiter, waitress, host, or hostess:

- **Back of the house** The kitchen and storage areas where the chefs, cooks, prep people, and dishwashers primarily work.
- **Double** Two shifts in a row: "I'm exhausted, I just pulled a double."
- **Push a dish** When you have a surplus of a certain ingredient or dish, the kitchen will often tell servers to recommend it. i.e. "Push the Cajun catfish—it won't be good tomorrow!"
- **Stiffed** Describes a server whose customer leaves without tipping.

How to Find a Job

Because the restaurant industry has such a fast turnover rate, positions waiting tables open regularly. If you come across as responsible, friendly, presentable, and quick-minded, you have a good chance of finding a job as a waiter or waitress. The most effective strategy simply to walk into a dozen or so restaurants in your neighborhood and introduce yourself to the manager; chances are you'll find at least one place that is looking for a new waiter or waitress. If this method sounds unappealing, however, there are Web sites, such as Craigslist.org and Monster.com that offer a venue for job listings, as does a few associations such as the American Hotel and Lodging Association, http://www.ahla.com

Once you've gained some experience, you may be able to move to a restaurant where there's a likelihood of a promotion to a position such as headwaiter or host or hostess. Restaurant managers are also often recruited from the ranks of experienced and competent waitstaff.

Secrets for Success

See the following suggestions and turn to the appendix for advice on résumés and interviews.

- ✴ Offer a smile! Friendliness is next to godliness in the service industry, so be sure to smile and be welcoming.
- ✴ Don't waste time. Efficiency is also key to succeeding in this business. It won't matter how nice you are if it takes you forever to serve drinks or ring up the check. Slow or forgetful waiters or waitresses can sacrifice their tips.

Reality Check

Though there is never a lack of food service jobs available, competition can be stiff, particularly in large cities. Job openings are often snatched up quickly by actors and other creative types attracted to the flexible hours. It's also important to remember that a lot of restaurants are looking for part-time workers, which isn't suitable for everyone. According to the Bureau of Labor Statistics, nearly half of the Americans who worked part-time jobs in 2004 were waiters and waitresses.

Some Other Jobs to Think About

- ✴ Retail Sales Assistant. As with waiting tables, a large part of retail involves serving customers and handling money. Friendliness, efficiency, and sharp social skills are prized skills in both professions.
- ✴ Caterer. Caterers work with food in social settings, which is similar to waiting tables or hostessing. The job also comes with a flexible schedule. However, caterers tend to work out of an office and spend a lot more time with their customers.

How You Can Move Up

- ✴ Put in those extra hours. The restaurant industry prides itself on being fast-paced and stress-inducing, so those who work hard and take on the double-shift are often rewarded.
- ✴ Show an interest in your customers and your coworkers. Restaurants, more so than many other businesses, are run like families,

so it's important to show you care about the food and how the establishment is being run. If you like a certain dish, let the kitchen and management know. Little things like this demonstrate a commitment and shows that you are part of the team.

★ Take a class. If you're invested in becoming a restaurant manager or owner one day, you'll want to take at least one class in food service management and accounting. Alternatively, you might want to consider taking some culinary courses.

Web Sites to Surf

National Restaurant Association. This is the leading association for the restaurant industry. Their Web site offers up-to-date industry facts as well as information on where to find jobs. http://www.restaurant.org

International Council on Hotel, Restaurant, and Institutional Education. One great way to better understand and appreciate the restaurant industry on an international level is to browse this Web site. It also offers tips on finding jobs. http://www.chrie.org

Meet interesting people

Bartender

Work in a relaxed and fun environment

Mix and create your own drinks

Bartender

Imagine knowing the secrets of mixing excellent mojitos, cosmopolitans, and other colorful or exotic cocktails. Imagine knowing the subtle differences among the best brands of scotch. Could you see yourself recommending pinot noir or cabernet, Amstel or Anchor Steam to an after-work crowd? As a bartender, you're a maestro of mixing, serving up drinks that your customers appreciate. Bars are one of the few places in the world where people can comfortably socialize with friends, business associates, or strangers. As a result, the atmosphere is often exciting and unpredictable. Apart from the busy periods, such as happy hour or the after-dinner crowd, the job is relatively stress-free. There's a reason why so many jokes begin with the phrase "a man walks into a bar . . ." Bartending can be fun, and the unexpected conversations you'll have with customers and coworkers can make the long hours and tiring work worthwhile.

Is This Job For You?

To find out if being a bartender is right for you, read each of the following statements and answer "Yes" or "No."

Yes	No	**1.**	Do you enjoy talking to a wide variety of people?
Yes	No	**2.**	Are you a fast and effective worker?
Yes	No	**3.**	Can you work in noisy environments?
Yes	No	**4.**	Do you have a good memory for drink proportions and names?
Yes	No	**5.**	Are you friendly and a good listener?
Yes	No	**6.**	Are you comfortable working late at night?
Yes	No	**7.**	Can you work on your feet for hours at a time?
Yes	No	**8.**	Are you assertive and able to deal with unruly customers?
Yes	No	**9.**	Are you trustworthy and able to handle money efficiently?
Yes	No	**10.**	Would you be able to resist drinking on the job?

If you answered "Yes" to most of the questions, you may have what it takes to be a bartender. To find out more about this profession, read on.

Let's Talk Money

Bartenders earn a median hourly wage of $7.42, or about $16,000 a year, according to 2006 data from the U.S. Bureau of Labor Statistics. However, this doesn't include tips, which can boost a bartender's income significantly. Bartenders working in swanky metropolitan bars frequented by big tippers can earn up to $60 an hour. If you're a bartender working a late shift in an upscale urban restaurant, you can make up to $600 a night. Like waiters and waitresses, bartenders may receive more than half of their earnings as tips.

What You'll Do

As a bartender, your main job is to fill drink orders from either customers at the bar or from waiters and waitresses delivering drinks to seated customers. Though this may sound routine, a surprising amount of focus and energy goes into preparing a well-mixed drink. From Singapore slings and sidecars to mud slides and martinis, you must know a wide range of drink recipes—and be able to mix them exactly. You may even create your own house specialty drinks. In addition to being fast, knowledgeable, and friendly, bartenders have a surprising amount of responsibility. They must keep tabs on how much everyone has been drinking, particularly if a person is alone or appears to be the designated driver. Bartenders must also check the identification of customers seated at the bar. Even though the legal drinking age in the United States is 21, bartenders should ask for identification from anyone who looks under the age of 25.

Drinks aside, there are a host of smaller tasks that bartenders manage. These include collecting money from customers seated at the bar, operating the cash register, and ordering and maintaining an inventory of liquors. In addition, you may be asked to wash glassware and utensils or serve food to customers seated at the bar.

Who You'll Work For

✴ Full-service and family owned restaurants
✴ Traditional bars and pubs
✴ Large-scale clubs or lounges

Let's Talk Money

Today there are about 474,000 bartenders serving drinks in the U.S., and job growth overall should be about average through 2014, according to the Bureau of Labor Statistics. However, jobs at upscale establishments are expected to increase at a faster rate due to the growing popularity of wine and fresh cocktails.

* Hotels, resorts, casinos, and cruise ships
* Sports arenas and certain other recreational facilities.
* Banquet halls
* Caterers

Where You'll Work

The majority of bartenders work behind a bar, where they serve and interact with patrons. This job requires you to be friendly and talkative, particularly if you want a good tip. Bartenders at service bars, on the other hand, have far less contact with customers. Service bars are usually small in size and located in the corners of restaurants, hotels, and clubs. Generally speaking, it's a place where waiters and waitresses place drink orders.

At large bars and clubs with high occupancy levels, some bartenders use equipment that automatically measures, pours, and mixes drinks at the push of a button, such as a margarita mixer. Bartenders who work in large bars may not do as much mixing, but they still must work quickly to handle a large volume of drink orders and be familiar with the ingredients for special drink requests. Regardless of where a bartender works, he or she will still have to fill drink orders by hand.

Your Typical Day

Here are typical highlights for a bartender working an evening shift.

✓ **Get in the saddle.** You arrive at about 4 p.m. Since most people are at work at this hour, you ease into your shift by wiping down the

The Inside Scoop: Q&A

Robert Cella
Bartender
Los Angeles, California

Q: *How did you get your job?*

A: The owner of Birds is a friend of mine. We used to tend bar side by side. When she and her husband told me that they were planning on opening a bar of their own, I said, "Let me know when that happens, and I'll come work for you." Two years later, they called to tell me that they'd bought a place. Every job I've landed was the result of knowing someone at that particular bar.

Q: *What do you like best about your job?*

A: I like that I can make a very comfortable living from a part-time job, and I don't "bring my work home with me." I'm also fortunate to work at Birds. Not every bar offers the earning potential of a recognized Hollywood tourist stop, but even a little neighborhood spot can offer a decent level of income.

Q: *What's the most challenging part of your job?*

A: The alcohol. It can be one of the most insidious substances on the planet. Dealing with it, and the consumers of it, can be both spiritually taxing and occasionally dangerous.

Q: *What are the keys to success to being a bartender?*

A: Don't abuse alcohol if you want to do this work successfully. I can't stress this enough. Another key to success is networking with other bartenders. You have to climb your own ladder of success in this industry. Many bartenders work at multiple places, and they can help get you in. Popular bars are more likely to hire a working bartender from another location if they are recommended by one of their employees. Many bartenders bounce from job to job until they find a bar that offers maximum return for their efforts.

bar, preparing margarita and mai tai mix, and making sure that there are enough clean glasses for the evening.

✔ **Make that one happy-but-hectic hour.** Happy hour or no happy hour, the busiest time for many bartenders is between 6 and 8 p.m. when the after-work crowd arrives. You may be taking up to five orders a minute, which can be overwhelming. On top of that, you'll have to keep track of multiple tabs and make sure that no one has had too much to drink.

✔ **Close out or burn the midnight oil.** Depending on your establishment's hours and clientele, either your customers will start to clear out by 10 p.m. or things may become chaotic. If you work in a restaurant bar, the crowd will start to wind down, and after washing some dishes, wiping down the bar, and doing some bottle inventory, you'll be able to leave. If you work at a late-night establishment, 1 to 2 a.m. will probably be your busiest hour.

What You Can Do Now

✦ If you're between 18 and 21 years of age, check to see what your state's minimum age to work as a bartender. Usually, bartenders must be at least 21, but in some states, you can start as early as 18. If you're of age, you should try finding part-time or seasonal work as a bartender.

✦ If you're under 18, you might want to try finding work as a bus boy, waiter, or waitress. Many people transition from waiting to bartending positions. Catering companies can also provide you with valuable experience. The summer and holiday season are the busiest times of year for catering companies, so caterers are always looking for high school or college students to fill in during these times.

✦ Do some research on the various restaurants, bars, and hotels in your area, and decide what sort of an establishment you'd like to work in. Once you've found a few places that interest you, introduce yourself to the manager or owner.

What Training You'll Need

Although some employers require you to have specialized training in food handling, most bartenders face no degree requirements for their job (although in some states they do face age requirements).

Employers are more likely to hire and promote based on people skills and personal qualities rather than on education. The most important training for bartending is practice. You might want to consider attending a bartending or technical school or take a class or two on mixing drinks. A bartending certificate takes only a few months to obtain, and it's a good credential to have, particularly if you want to bartend at a high-end bar, hotel, or restaurant. Programs often include instruction on state and local laws and regulations, cocktail recipes, proper attire and conduct, and stocking a bar. Some of these schools also help their graduates find jobs. In addition to attending school, you if you want to work at a nightclub or trendy bar, you might want to take a one-day or online TIPs (training for intervention procedures) course, designed to show you how to prevent intoxication and manage intoxicated customers. As the number of liquor-related lawsuits continues to grow, bars and nightclubs are starting to require their bartenders to take a TIPs course.

How to Talk Like A Pro

Here are a few words that bartenders throw around on the job:

- **Call drink** A drink in which the customer asks for a specific brand of alcohol by name; these are almost always more expensive than regular drinks.
- **Nightcap** A glass of wine or liquor ingested before bedtime.
- **Nip** A term of measurement used to describe a quarter of a bottle. In the old days, people were known to have "a nipper" of brandy or another liquor before bed.
- **On the rocks** An expression for serving a drink on ice cubes; contrasts with "neat," which calls for serving a liquor pure—with no water or ice.
- **Twist** A small piece of lemon or lime peel that is squeezed over a drink.
- **Proof** An American system for measuring alcohol content by volume. The proof of a liquor is always marked on the bottle and is twice the pure alcohol percentage of the distillation. For example, there is a particularly strong Bacardi line of rum called 151, which refers to the 151 proof of the liquor, or its containing more than 75 percent pure alcohol.

How to Find a Job

Thankfully, you don't need to be Tom Cruise in *Cocktail* to find work as a bartender. There is a preponderance of bartending jobs available in the United States. However, it's a popular profession, so jobs are often snatched up quickly. In order to snag one, you must be tenacious. Don't be afraid to walk into a bar or restaurant and hand the owner your résumé. It's important to remember that since the job requires little or no training, how you appear in person is just as important as how you appear on paper. A sunny and difficult-to-rattle disposition goes a long way in bartending. If you are disinclined to drop into a restaurant or bar unannounced, you may find a bartending job by checking online or city bulletin boards and though word of mouth. Internet sites such as Craigslist.org and Monster.com are good resources. However, if you do decide to drop off your résumé, make sure you give it to the owner or bar manager instead of the current bartender, who might be reluctant to pass it along.

Secrets for Success

See the following suggestions and turn to the appendix for advice on résumés and interviews.

- ✵ Talk 'em up. Although a friendly and winsome personality is technically not a job requirement, it certainly helps, particularly if you want to make good tips and develop a loyal clientele. Whenever you have some downtime, make an effort to chat with your customers at the bar and make sure that they are happy with their drinks.
- ✵ Know the law. Most important, be sure you know the state and local laws concerning the sale of alcoholic beverages. Serving liquor to a minor can result in the closing of a bar. In some states you might also be responsible for the actions of an intoxicated customer who drinks on your premises.

Reality Check

Bartenders at some establishments are required to "upsell," meaning to push customers to buy additional drinks or appetizers. The selling aspect of this job is not for everyone.

Some Other Jobs to Think About

✴ Waiter/waitress or host/hostess. Like bartending, these jobs require you to work in similar environments and to be be fast, fas-
tidious, and friendly. For a more complete description of what
goes into waiting and hostessing, see Chapter 2.

✴ Sommelier. After working as a bartender for a few years, some
people become very passionate about wine. Sommeliers are wine
experts who are hired by upscale restaurants order wines and to
help customers select wines that will compliment their palates
and their meals.

How You Can Move Up

✴ Create your own concoctions. Experimentation and innovation
can go a long way in the bartending business, so don't be afraid
to create and name your own drinks. Owners and managers are
often impressed with ingenuity, and customers like to try a new
house specialty drink.

✴ Take a class. If you decide you really enjoy bartending, get your
bartending license and take at least one class in food service
management and accounting. Alternatively, you might want to
consider taking some culinary courses.

✴ Schmooze. The word may sound silly, but in the bartending
business getting to know your customers may help you land you
a promotion or a better-paying job elsewhere, or connect you
with an opportunity in some other area of your interests.

✴ Be a manager. Take on additional responsibilities for the restaurant or bar where you work, such as maintaining the staff
schedule, and you are likely to be promoted to manager.

Web Sites to Surf

Extreme Bartending. This is a fun and informative site that offers information on the latest mixing tricks and trends. It also provides valuable tips on
how to find jobs in the field.   http//:www.extremebartending.com

American Hotel and Lodging Association. This site has a great job search en-
gine that's updated on a consistent basis and easy to use.
http://www.ahla.com/index.asp

Design floral displays and bouquets

Floral Arranger

Add color and happiness to others' lives

Design floral displays and bouquets

Floral Arranger

Gertrude Stein once wrote, "A rose is a rose is a rose." Though this may be true for the average person, a florist knows there are more than 100 different wild rose species in the Northern Hemisphere alone. Florists are nature's salespeople. They cut live flowers and greenery and arrange them into beautiful displays. It's a wonderfully creative job that adds color and joy to people's lives. It's also a job that is growing in popularity. Nowadays, almost every major occasion in life calls for a flower display of some sort. Think about it: weddings, funerals, promotions, prom night, performances, Valentine's Day, and Christmas all involve flowers or greenery of some sort. With so many occasions for flowers, it's no wonder there are close to 100,000 florists in the United States.

Is This Job for You?

To find out if being a floral arranger could be the right job for you, read each of the following questions and answer "Yes" or "No."

Yes	No	**1.**	Are you creative, and do you have an eye for color and composition?
Yes	No	**2.**	Are you patient and detail-oriented?
Yes	No	**3.**	Are you passionate about flowers?
Yes	No	**4.**	Do you enjoy working with your hands?
Yes	No	**5.**	Would you enjoy learning about the qualities of hundreds of floral varieties?
Yes	No	**6.**	Are you comfortable working weekends and holidays?
Yes	No	**7.**	Do you work well under pressure?
Yes	No	**8.**	Are you friendly and personable?
Yes	No	**9.**	Can you work well both independently and with others?
Yes	No	**10.**	Can you interpret other's design needs and preferences?

If you answered "Yes" to most or all of these questions, you may want to consider a career as a floral arranger. To find out more about this job, read on.

Let's Talk Money

Floral designers earn a median annual income of about $20,450, according to 2006 data from the U.S. Bureau of Labor Statistics. However, those who manage their own stores often make substantially more.

What You'll Do

As a florist, you are required to be both an artist and a listener. When a customer walks in the store, a good florist will talk to the person to figure out how to convey just the right message with a floral arrangement. Once the right bouquet or display has been chosen, a florist must price the order and give the customer a time estimate. After this is accomplished, the florist can put together the arrangement. Florists may also receive written or online orders, which do not require customer contact. This is particularly common at large retail stores and Internet florists.

However, most florists today still work in small storefront shops with 10 or fewer employees. Whether you're self-employed or working in a small florist shop, you will frequently work independently, so you should be a self-sufficient and disciplined worker. You will likely also handle large orders for weddings, caterers, or interior designers. These jobs often require florists to put in extra hours and to go onsite to arrange bouquets and floral displays. Seasoned florists are also asked to collaborate with interior designers on major design projects for hotels, restaurants, and private homes.

Who You'll Work For

- ✴ Small flower shops
- ✴ Florist chains, such as 1-800-FLOWERS
- ✴ Wholesalers
- ✴ Large grocery stores
- ✴ Online flower companies, such as www.dotflowers.com

Where You'll Work

Although job environments in the floral industry vary, many florists still work in small, independently run shops with a strong repeat-client base. To supplement their store income, many florists also run gift shops or wedding consultation businesses.

If you aren't a self-employed florist or employed at an independent flower shop, you may work for a wholesale flower distribution company. Wholesale florists select different varieties of flowers and greenery and sell them to retail florists. This job requires an intimate knowledge of the industry, as well as a sharp eye.

In recent years, the Internet flower industry has also started to flourish, and as a result, a growing number of people are seeking employment in this area. As an Internet florist, your job is to create prearranged floral bouquets and displays. Although the job doesn't involve much creativity or collaboration, you won't have to deal with persnickety clients.

These days many people are picking up their flowers at large grocery chain. Florists also work designing and creating the arrangements at large distribution centers. However, such a position is much more routine and doesn't offer much chance for self-expression.

Your Typical Day

Here are the highlights of a typical day in a floral shop.

✔ **Brighten up the shop.** Arrange a few fresh bouquets or topiaries for the storefront window. Once the shop is looking brighter, you'll want to prearrange a few fresh bouquets for customers who are in a hurry. The morning is also a good time to call distributors and schedule deliveries.

✔ **Dote on your customers.** Chat with those who stop by the store to find out the reason they are shopping for flowers and what sort of flowers they appreciate. Once you know the occasion and the customer's likes and dislikes, you'll be able to arrange something unique and appropriate for them.

Let's Talk Trends

The number of florists in the United States has blossomed in the past decade, in part because weddings and funerals have both grown increasingly expensive and elaborate. Today there are close to 100,000 florists in the United States, and this figure is expected to grow through 2014, according to the Bureau of Labor Statistics.

✔ **Clean up and close the store.** After store hours, you'll need to close the register and sweep up any petals or leaves from the floor. Before leaving, it's always a good idea to see what deliveries are scheduled for the next day.

What You Can Do Now

✯ Borrow a few flower-arranging books from your local library or take a floral design class. Then buy an assortment of flowers and practice putting together handheld bouquets, corsages, or arrangements for containers. Once you've mastered the basics, you can move on to advanced concepts in floral design, such as horizontal, landscape, and waterfall style.

✯ Pay attention in Bio! If you're no longer in school, take a botany or horticulture class. Most colleges offer horticulture courses, and some community centers have evening classes in botany or flower appreciation.

✯ Try finding part-time or volunteer work at a local florist. Even if you're just delivering flowers, you'll eventually learn the great arrangement for every occasion.

What Training You'll Need

On-the-job training is a good way to gain an understanding of the floristry business. It's also the best way to develop your own style and figure out what particular type of floral design (funeral wreaths, topiaries, bouquets) suits you best. Floral design is one of the few design occupations that doesn't require a postsecondary education, so many florists are high school graduates who have a creative flair and an interest in the arts as well as nature.

However, those who do have formal training in floral design tend to have a leg up on the competition. If you're interested in opening your own store or becoming a hot-shot floral designer, you might want to consider a floral school or a community college that awards certificates in floral design. These programs are usually inexpensive and can be completed in one year or less. Through them you'll learn the basics in floral design: the different species of flowers, their color and texture, cutting and taping techniques, and proper handling and care of flowers. Many programs will also teach you the elements of running your own floral business, from pricing to bookkeeping.

The Inside Scoop: Q&A

Janell Arce
Floral arranger and store manager
Austin, Texas

Q: *How did you get your job?*

A: I had interviews with other floral shops, but ultimately I felt that the King Florist team would give me the opportunity to excel in the floral industry. When you're first starting out, it's important to interview with a lot of florists. Since most businesses are small, it's important to pick the work environment that suits you best. At King Florist, I started as a general staff member, and after two years of writing down orders and arranging flowers, I was promoted to shop manager.

Q: *What do you like best about your job?*

A: It's wonderful to be around flowers, and to use your creativity at the workplace every day. It's also nice to have a customer appreciate your work. People are often fascinated by the many ways in which we can present flowers, so I love seeing their reaction when they receive a bouquet that was created and designed just for them.

Q: *What's the most challenging part of your job?*

A: Dealing with new or demanding clients can sometimes be difficult. Also, when a potential client calls, you only have a few minutes to sell them on the fact that King Florist is a trusted name. Since flower shops are small and friendly, it's easy to forget that we are in the sales business. For some people, the selling part of the job can be difficult.

Q: *What are the keys to success to being a florist?*

A: Apart from strong customer service skills, the biggest key to success in this business is consistency and a distinguished style. If you consistently create floral designs that appeal to your clientele, and noticeably set you apart from the flower shop around the corner, you should be in business for a long time.

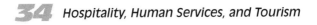

How to Talk Like a Pro

Here are a few words that you're likely to hear on the job:

- ✴ **Oasis** Special foam used in flower arrangements. It retains water like a sponge and hydrates flowers for an extended period of time.
- ✴ **Topiary** Flowers or foliage trimmed into geometric shapes. The design often resembles miniature trees or animals.
- ✴ **Nosegays** Small, round bouquets that are composed of densely packed round flowers, greenery, and occasionally herbs. Nosegays are either wired or tied together.

How to Find a Job

Despite the corporatization of America, for the most part, the flower industry is still a cottage industry. One out of three florists in the United States is self-employed and works in a quaint storefront shop. If you're interested in running your own floral business, start by going to your local flower district and have a look around. Once you feel familiar with the regional flowers and their pricing, consider buying several dozen different flowers, obtaining a wholesale license (license prices vary state by state but usually cost about $2 per day) and opening up a stand. If you don't have the clientele or the overhead to start your own store, this is the best way to make money and get to know your client base. If, on the other hand, you're interested in working on the corporate side of the industry, a number of online and wholesale flower companies now offer internships.

Secrets for Success

See the following suggestions and turn to the appendix for advice on résumés and interviews.

- ✴ Since flowers are all about presentation, it's important to smile and present yourself in a pleasant way. A good florist knows the right flowers for the right occasion, and to pick the right bouquet or floral display, you need to be able to listen and interpret the needs of your client. After all, you wouldn't want to sell a Venus flytrap to a man who's about to propose.

✴ Learn about color—design books can be a good place to start. The color composition of a bouquet determines a lot of what it expresses.

Reality Check

Flowers may be pretty, but unfortunately, the same can't be said for the flower industry. Flower shops rely on word of mouth, and some clients take advantage of this fact. As a result, florists often have to go to great efforts to please and appease their clients.

Some Other Jobs to Think About

✴ Horticulture assistant. This occupation allows you to work with flora and fauna in nurseries or elsewhere. These workers usually have regular hours, but they are often laboring outdoors in hot weather for long periods of time.

✴ Fashion designer. As with flower arranging, fashion design requires you to have a good eye for color and composition. However, fashion design is an extremely competitive area and typically requires more education.

How You Can Move Up

✴ Take a horticulture class at a local college or community center. At the very least, read books and watch videos on floral design and botany and start memorizing the many different species of flowers that are available through your wholesalers or locally.

✴ Learn all you can about the wholesale flower distribution business. Even if you have no interest in working as a flower distributor, this is a great way to learn about the flower industry. Consider volunteering as a intern or taking a part-time job in this area to solidify your knowledge.

✴ Be quick to volunteer for additional responsibilities at your job. Come in during rush periods, be willing to fill in for others, and generally make yourself indispensable—especially with regard to management tasks.

✴ Take business courses at a local community college and learn all you can about running your own business or managing others.

Web Sites to Surf

American Institute of Floral Designers (AIFD). This is one of the best networking resources for florists. Their Web site tracks the latest floral trends and often features floral events, job opportunities, workshops, and symposia. http://www.aifd.org

Flowerchat.com. Flower Chat is a great site to visit if you are new to the industry and would like to speak with florists from around the country. With a membership of over 2,000, it offers plenty of experts who are willing to field questions and help you get started.   http://www.flowerchat.com

Work in a social environment

Launderer
or
Dry Cleaner

Expose yourself to fashion styles

Make clothes smell fresh and please customers

Launderer or Dry Cleaner

Being a dry cleaner is one of the most overlooked fashion-related careers. Though it may not be as glamorous as designing couture clothes, the work is steady, and there is a great demand for dry cleaners. People of almost every age and income use laundry and dry cleaning services, which is why such businesses can be found in virtually every American town and city. Moreover, there is more to dry cleaning than just removing stains and spots—a lot of hard work and responsibility goes into running a laundry and dry cleaning business.

As a dry cleaner, you are responsible for people's most cherished articles of clothing. You also are under a lot of deadlines. It is not uncommon for someone to come into the store with a tuxedo that needs to be cleaned by tomorrow or a tie that needs a stain removed for a dinner that evening. It's a demanding job, but there is a great amount of satisfaction involved. It's also relatively easy to start your own laundry and dry cleaning business. So if you're a clean and careful worker who enjoys clothing and wants to run a small business, this may be the position for you.

Is This Job For You?

To find out if being a laundry or dry cleaning worker is a good fit for you, read each of the following statements and answer "Yes" or "No."

Yes	*No*	**1.**	Do you enjoy working with fabrics and cloth?
Yes	*No*	**2.**	Are you good at budgeting your time?
Yes	*No*	**3.**	Can you work weekends or evenings?
Yes	*No*	**4.**	Are you capable of being on your feet all day?
Yes	*No*	**5.**	Are you a strong, independent worker?
Yes	*No*	**6.**	Do you not have allergies to chemicals or perfumes, or can you manage them?
Yes	*No*	**7.**	Might you be interested in running a business?
Yes	*No*	**8.**	Do you have an appreciation for fashion?
Yes	*No*	**9.**	Are you a neat person who values cleanliness?
Yes	*No*	**10.**	Are you friendly, and could you attract a loyal client base?

If you answered "Yes" to most of the questions, you may be well-suited to work as a dry cleaner. To find out more about this profession, read on.

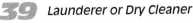

Let's Talk Money

The median hourly earnings for laundry and dry cleaning workers are about $8.28 per hour, or about $17,000 a year, according to 2006 figures from the U.S. Bureau of Labor Statistics. Self-employed dry cleaners or workers covered by union contracts tend to generate a larger income.

What You'll Do

As a laundry or dry cleaning worker, your responsibility is to launder, clean, dye, and press an ongoing stream of articles—from clothing, linens, and bedding to curtains, drapes, and rugs. Though this may seem like a simple task, dry cleaning is actually a rather intricate and mysterious process. One of the biggest myths about dry cleaning is that the process is entirely dry. Actually, dry cleaning uses a variety of different non-water-based solvents to remove stains and clean clothes. The solvent is placed inside a dry cleaning machine, which acts as both a washing machine and dryer.

As a dry cleaner, it is your job to monitor the machine and adjust the temperatures according to the color and fabric of the materials. It is also your job to ensure that a customer's item is not lost or misplaced. Like most jobs in human services, customer satisfaction is essential to the business. In addition to being fast and efficient, you must also be friendly and courteous. Whether it's an expensive designer garment or someone's favorite pair of blue jeans, clients trust their dry cleaner to remove spots, repair hems, and make sure those garments are looking their best. The personal component of the job is particularly important if you're the manager or owner of the business.

Laundry and dry cleaning stores are steady and reliable business enterprises, which is why many budding business owners open dry cleaning businesses. There is a strong entrepreneurial element in the laundry and dry cleaning industry. Not only can you open a store almost anywhere, as the owner you get to decide what services to offer. Offering additional services, such as tailoring, same-day home delivery, or environmentally "green" cleaning processes is a good way for owners to separate themselves from the competition.

Laundry and dry cleaning establishments usually have one manager and at least three employees. There is also an owner, but in

Let's Talk Trends

As long as people feel the need to wear clean clothes, there will always be a need for launderers and dry cleaners. It's a timeless profession, which is why employment figures remain relatively steady. As of 2007, there are close to 235,000 laundry and dry-cleaning workers in the United States alone.

many cases the owner and manager are one and the same. It's important to know that a lot of laundry and dry cleaning businesses are family-run. This often close-knit family dynamic can create a warm and intimate work environment for some, but it can also make others feel like an outsider.

As for your clientele, it's usually very diverse. Though office workers tend to need shirts pressed and skirts cleaned on a more regular basis, almost everyone has a need for dry cleaning at some point. Thus, as a dry cleaner, you'll be able to meet and serve a diverse group of customers.

Who You'll Work For

✯ A small business owner
✯ Yourself

Where You'll Work

One of the best parts about being in the laundry and dry cleaning business is that you can find work wherever you live. Laundry and dry cleaning establishments are found in throughout the nation, so if you want to settle down in a small town, just find a business partner or gather up some money on your own. Or, if you crave the culture and entertainment that places like Los Angeles or New York have to offer, you can make a decent living running your own laundry and dry cleaning shop in a big city.

One thing to keep in mind is that laundry and dry cleaning establishments typically make most of their money during the evening and on weekends, so weekend and evening shifts are pretty standard. Some managers or owners rotate schedules so that employees do not continuously work nights or weekends, but this can cause sleep disorders or other aggravations.

The Inside Scoop: Q&A

Stephen Hong
Dry cleaning business manager
Bloomfield, New Jersey

Q: *How did you get your job?*

A: My parents owned a dry cleaning business, so it was a way for me to spend time with my parents. I would stop by and help out after school and on Saturdays. That's how it started. As I grew up, I just took over the business from my parents.

Q: *What do you like best about your job?*

A: Dry cleaners attract local business, so as a dry cleaner, you get to know your neighbors. You would be amazed at how much you learn about people and life just by speaking with customers and taking care of their clothes on a regular basis.

Q: *What's the most challenging part of your job?*

A: Trying to remove stains from customer's clothes—it is amazing what people get on their clothes. They also think that dry cleaners can remove every stain, but sometimes that's just not possible, particularly if you have a wine or ink stain on a white, absorbent fabric.

Q: *What are the keys to success to being a dry cleaner?*

A: The three main keys to success in this business are: quality, maintenance, and customer service. High-quality dry cleaning makes clothes look and feel like you just bought them. Equipment maintenance is also essential. If one of your machines breaks down you cannot do any work until it's fixed. The final key to success is customer service. Without good customer service, you are bound to fail in this or any other business.

Your Typical Day

Ever wonder what a dry cleaner does with your clothes once you leave? As a dry cleaner, you'll spend a great deal of your day doing the following.

✔ **Tag and sort.** You'll affix a small identification tag to the customer's clothing. The tag helps distinguish the clothes, and so it remains attached to the clothing during the entire dry-cleaning cycle.

✔ **Run the machines.** You or a colleague will put the clothing into a machine to be cleaned with a powerful solvent. Most modern machines are a washer, extractor, and dryer all in one and can hold between 20 to 100 pounds of clothing or fabric.

✔ **Post-spot those stains!** This process involves using a variety of equipment and chemicals to get particular stains out. Water-based stains such as tomato sauce are removed using steam or wet-side chemicals. Other stains (grease or nail polish) are removed using solvents or dry-side chemicals.

✔ **Finish up.** To get a garment or item is ready for the customer, you either press, fold, and package, or oversee this process.

What You Can Do Now

✴ Each laundry and dry cleaning establishment is slightly different. Research some of the specialized services, such as bridal-gown cleaning, corporate dry cleaning, and "green" processes, and decide which ones interest you most.

✴ Take chemistry classes to familiarize yourself with the properties of the chemicals used in the dry cleaning process.

✴ Look for part-time or weekend work at a local laundry or dry cleaning establishment. Even if you're just pressing shirts or sweeping up lint, you'll get a good sense of how the business works.

What Training You'll Need

On-the-job training is the best way to break into this business. Although employers prefer applicants to have previous work experience, laundry and dry cleaning managers routinely hire inexperienced workers. Often an owner or manager will have you shadow another employee for a week, so you can learn the basic procedures. After that, you're on your own. College degrees, business management experience, or dry-cleaning training certificates will definitely set you apart from the competition, but a high school diploma is all that's really needed in order to work at a dry cleaning establishment.

Though most states require dry cleaning businesses to be certified, employees typically do not need any form of certification. There are, however, week- or month-long courses that teach the basic principles of the dry cleaning process, stain removal, and finishing procedures on pants, coats, and skirts. These courses also cover some business basics, such as assembly and invoicing as well as regulations and care labeling.

If you're planning on opening a laundry or dry cleaning shop someday, it's a good idea to take courses in both business and fabric maintenance. Dry cleaning also deals with hazardous chemicals, which can pollute the environment if employees are not careful. In an effort to keep our air clean, a lot of states have now imposed environmental training regulations. These courses will give you a brief history of dry cleaning solvents, and teach you how to prevent toxic leaks and environmental damage through recordkeeping and rigorous maintenance checks. Regardless of whether your state requires you to take environmental courses, it is essential that you know study up on the hazardous effects of perchloroethylene (perc) and the other solvents used during the cleaning process.

How to Talk Like a Pro

Here are a few words you're likely to hear as a laundry or dry cleaning worker:

- **Perchloroethylene (perc)** This solvent is the standard for cleaning performance. It's a very aggressive cleaner that can cause color loss if it is not used properly and at the right temperature.
- **Pre-treatment** This is a technique in which a cleaner uses chemicals to remove or minimize a stain before the dry cleaning process.
- **The basket** Also known as the washing/extracting chamber, the basket is the core of the dry cleaning machine. It's comprised of a shell, which holds the solvent, and a rotating drum, which can hold between 20 to 100 pounds of garments.
- **Filter cake (aka muck)** This accumulates on the surface of the lint filter. The muck must be removed once per day, and then filtered to recover any solvent trapped in the muck.

How to Find a Job

To find a job in the laundry or dry cleaning business, call or stop by businesses for whom you think you'd like to work. Remember, there are dry cleaning businesses in almost every town, so you'll probably have at least several options. Be sure to research all the stores in your surrounding area. Remember that dry cleaners prefer efficient, friendly, and presentable people, so press your shirt before going into an interview and be sure to greet everyone with a smile. Most facilities will offer training, so you needn't worry about your experience level. Dry cleaning stores have a consistent turnover rate, so if you can't find a job at your favorite dry cleaner, check back every few weeks or months. Another point to keep in mind is that dry cleaners are often busier on weekends and during the holiday season, so asking for part-time work during these times is an option.

Secrets for Success

See the following suggestions and turn to the appendix for advice on résumés and interviews.

- Look professional. People launder and dry clean their clothes because they want to look clean and presentable; so as the dry cleaner, it is important for you to look polished and presentable too.
- Don't cut corners. Equally important is the quality of your services, which depends largely on the degree to which you control the dry cleaning machine's filter, solvent condition, and moisture. Therefore it is important to pay careful attention to the machines and perform maintenance work on them when necessary.

Reality Check

Laundry and dry cleaning establishments are often hot and noisy, so if you are looking for a quiet work environment, this may not be the job for you. In addition, injuries are not uncommon because some of the solvents used are flammable and the machines operate at high speeds.

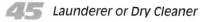

Some Other Jobs to Think About

✳ Cobbler. Cobblers repair shoes and work in the same sorts of small storefronts as favored by dry cleaners. The customer contact may be less regular because shoes stay fixed longer than clothes stay clean, but many find this old-world craft a very fulfilling occupation.

✳ Upholsterer. Upholsterers work closely with customers in repairing furniture and making it from scratch. They work a lot with their hands, and have to be competent with numbers as there are many separate pieces that must come together to form a whole.

How You Can Move Up

✳ One of the best ways to establish yourself is to take part in community activities. You'd be amazed at how much business you can drum up just by being an active member of the community. If you own your own business, your profits can be increased substantially by adding new services, such as boxing and storing, home delivery, alteration services, and coin machine laundering.

✳ Once you know the business, another option is to open several dry cleaning outlets with a central locale for the dry cleaning processes.

Web Sites to Surf

Drycleaning & Laundry Institute. This Web site offers vital and up-to-date information about the garment-cleaning industry. For institute members, there are forums, contact lists, online seminars, and invitations to conferences. http://www.ifi.org

National Cleaners Association (NCA). This is a great trade organization that services garment-cleaning businesses both large and small. Headquartered in New York City, the NCA offers scholarships and can put you in touch with industry experts. Check your state association's site as well. http://www.nca-i.com

GreenEarth Cleaning. This site offers information on environmentally cleaner, Perc-free dry cleaning processes, as well as other information, and its "green" dry cleaners by city and state. http://www.greenearth cleaning.com

Travel the world

Flight Attendant

Shape passengers' flying experiences

Meet interesting and diverse people

Flight Attendant

Imagine traveling all across the continent or throughout the world. Flight attendants get these exciting opportunities. What's more, they also meet a huge range of passengers, from parents flying internationally to meet a soon-to-be adopted infant to a chief executive on his or her way to a multimillion dollar deal. A flight attendant's job is to keep everyone on board safe and comfortable. Though passengers may be mainly aware of their flight attendants' duties pointing out emergency exits and making sure that carry-on items are properly stowed, in fact that's just a small part of what they do. They are an important part of air security, and have a serious job that requires patience, endurance, and energy. As it happens, the benefits are enticing. Flight attendants receive plenty of time off, and they and their immediate family members often get enormous discounts on airfare, allowing attendants to travel widely in their free time.

Is This Job For You?

To find out if being a flight attendant is a good fit for you, read each of the following questions and answer "Yes" or "No."

Yes	*No*	**1.**	Do you like to travel, and are you unafraid of flying?
Yes	*No*	**2.**	Do you remain calm under duress?
Yes	*No*	**3.**	Are you poised, patient, and presentable?
Yes	*No*	**4.**	Can you assert yourself and take charge when necessary?
Yes	*No*	**5.**	Do you enjoy talking to strangers?
Yes	*No*	**6.**	Do you prefer a varied work schedule?
Yes	*No*	**7.**	Are you a good listener?
Yes	*No*	**8.**	Do you enjoy working on your feet, and are you physically fit?
Yes	*No*	**9.**	Could you work in a confined space for long stretches of time?
Yes	*No*	**10.**	Are in interested in the well-being and comfort of others?

If you answered "Yes" to most of the questions, you may have what it takes to be a flight attendant. To find out more about this profession, read on.

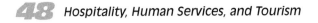

Let's Talk Money

Flight attendants earn a median salary of $43,440, according to 2006 data from the U.S. Bureau of Labor Statistics. However, the pay scale for flight attendants varies by greatly by carrier and a flight attendant's level of experience. New attendants only earned an average of $15,552, while the highest 10 percent of flight attendants made more than $95,850, according to the Association of Flight Attendants (AFA).

What You'll Do

Regardless of what airline you work for, a flight attendant's primary responsibility is to ensure the safety of his or her passengers. Airlines are required by law to enforce certain safety regulations, such as fastening seat belts and making sure that there is no smoking on board. It is the flight attendant's job to ensure that all in-flight rules and regulations are followed.

Flight attendants spend a considerable amount of time providing customers with drinks and duty-free items, so passengers tend to forget the importance of a flight attendant's job. In many ways, flight attendants are the unsung heroes of the air. During rough weather conditions, they care for sick or anxious passengers. They also administer first aid to passengers who become ill onboard, and if the pilots need to make an emergency landing, it is the attendant who directs the evacuation.

In addition to serving the passengers and making sure that safety procedures are being followed, flight attendants have paperwork and administrative tasks to fulfill. Prior to landing, attendants must take inventory of headsets, alcoholic beverages, and moneys collected. They also must write a quick report detailing the condition of the cabin, any items left behind, and if there were any incidents or medical problems on board. If you thought that a flight attendant's job was just to look good and pour coffee, you might want to think again.

Who You'll Work For

✴ Commercial airline companies, such as Delta, American Airlines, or Virgin Air.

✶ Fractional jet companies such as NetJets, which specialize in timeshare planes.

✶ Major corporations and companies, which operate aircraft for business purposes.

Where You'll Work

It goes without saying that flight attendants spend a significant portion of their workday confined in an aircraft. Because airlines fly 24/7, flight attendants may work nights, holidays, and weekends. Scheduled on-duty time is usually limited to 12 hours per day, but it can be longer if you work for an international carrier.

In addition to the time spent in flight, attendants generally spend about 50 hours a month on the ground preparing planes for flights, writing reports, and waiting for planes to arrive. Generally speaking, flight attendants will work three-day sequences and then receive three or four days off. You can use this time to start a second business or take advantage of the incredible travel benefits that airlines offer flight attendants.

As far as housing is concerned, airlines will assign you to one of their home bases, so most flight attendants choose to live in a town or city that's near to their assigned base. Since home bases and routes are chosen on a seniority basis, the longer you've been employed, the more likely you are to receive your desired route. Most beginning flight attendants work on call, which means that they must be willing to relocate in a relatively short period of time.

This job requires you to be flexible with your hours and to be willing to relocate. It can also be exhausting, but most attendants feel that the job is worth it. Not only does the job offer you great traveling opportunities, but as a flight attendant you are the most visible representative of airline companies. Airlines count on you to build customer relations and maintain their image.

Let's Talk Trends

Flight attendants held more than 102,000 jobs in 2004. This figure is expected to grow with the introduction of more charter airline companies. In addition, many corporations are looking for professionally trained attendants to work on their private aircraft.

Your Typical Day

Here are the highlights of a typical flight attendant's day.

- ✓ **Meet with other crew members.** The captain will gather you and your fellow flight attendants to go over such details as the approximate length of the flight, expected weather conditions, and special issues having to do with passengers.
- ✓ **Direct the boarding of the craft.** You'll greet passengers, check their tickets, and tell them where to store carry-on items. You'll also give the emergency equipment demonstration, and check to see that seatbelts are fastened, seat backs are in upright positions, and all carry-on items are properly stowed.
- ✓ **Serve simple needs and be ready for more.** You'll provide passengers with in-flight meals, drinks, duty-free items, and headsets for in-flight entertainment. If there is an injury on board or someone falls ill, the passengers are your responsibility.

What You Can Do Now

- ✦ Learn as much as you can about in-flight safety.
- ✦ Pay attention in language class! Flight attendants interested in working for international airlines must speak at least one foreign language.
- ✦ Hiring policies differ from airline to airline, so it's a good idea to search the Web sites of individual airlines to check out their job opportunities and application requirements.

What Training You'll Need

Although a high school diploma or its equivalent is technically all that's required to enter a flight attendant training program, airlines increasingly prefer applicants with customer service experience or some degree of postsecondary education.

If you're planning to take classes toward an associate or bachelor's degree before becoming a flight attendant, airlines look for applicants who have studied public service disciplines such as psychology, communications, social studies, or education. Studying a foreign language will also set you apart from the competition. Airlines actively recruit bilingual applicants.

The Inside Scoop: Q&A

Joyce Peterson
Flight attendant
New York, New York

Q: *How did you get your job?*

A: I walked into a Delta ticket office in New York City. At the office, they had me fill out an application, and then I flew to Atlanta for an interview with both Delta's people and a psychiatrist (they like to make sure that you aren't unstable). The rest is history.

Q: *What do you like best about your job?*

A: The best part is the people and the amazing travel opportunities. Being involved with the airline industry is not just a job, it's a lifestyle. I'm gone from home quite a bit, but the people I work with have a wonderful sense of adventure. I feel very fortunate to be able to visit places like Paris, Rome, and Mumbai. I also really enjoy the fact that we work in an environment where no one is looking over your shoulder.

Q: *What's the most challenging part of your job?*

A: Onboard, long flights can be stressful, especially when you're in tight quarters or a passenger has had too much to drink. Alcohol has a much stronger affect on people at higher altitudes, and once in a while people get out of control. After September 11, traveling has become more difficult for everyone, and the airport scene can be particularly stressful. Another challenge is dealing with jetlag. When you disrupt your circadian rhythms on a regular basis, it can wreak havoc on your sleep cycle. I have become an expert at taking power naps. Exercise also helps.

Q: *What are the keys to success to being a flight attendant?*

A: Success in this field involves a sense of humor and flexibility. At 35,000 feet, you have to be creative and quick to solve problems as they arise. People will present you with all kinds of situations, and while it's important to take their needs seriously, you also need to find humor in some of the more difficult demands.

For those who do not wish to start an associate's or bachelor's degree, there are training schools and online programs that offer courses on becoming a flight attendant. The objective of these courses is to go over basic in-flight safety procedures and prepare students for the rigorous application process that airlines impose on flight attendant applicants.

One of the most rigorous parts of the application process is the background check, which the FAA (Federal Aviation Administration) now requires of all applicants. Everything about an applicant is investigated, including date of birth, employment history, criminal record, school records, and gaps in employment. If an applicant's background check reveals any major inconsistencies, an applicant will not be offered a job or will be immediately dismissed from the training program.

After passing the the interview and background checks, applicants are entered into the airline's flight attendant training program, which can take three to eight weeks. Training programs differ from airline to airline, but every program covers fundamental emergency procedures, such as how to evacuate an airplane, administer first aid, survive in the water, and handle a terrorist situation. Before graduating from the program, you must successfully complete emergency and nonemergency drills. Once you accomplish all this, you will officially receive a certificate of demonstrated proficiency from the FAA, and the airline will assign you to one of their bases.

How to Talk Like a Pro

Here are a few words you're likely to hear as a flight attendant:

- ✴ **City codes** These are the abbreviations for the airports in U.S. and international cities. Most airlines require flight attendants to memorize at least several dozen airport codes, such as LAX (Los Angeles International Airport), DUB (Dublin), HKG (Hong Kong), and JFK (New York's John F. Kennedy Airport).
- ✴ **Hub** The city in which an airline is based and has its headquarters. Typically, this is where many transfer flights for a particular airline occur as well as flight attendant training.
- ✴ **Pre-flight briefing** This is the safety demonstration given to airline passengers before takeoff. It often features a public address in which flight attendants show how to inflate an aircraft life vest.

How to Find a Job

Competition for flight attendant positions is always high, thanks to the great travel opportunities available to attendants. Airlines are looking for highly presentable and poised men and women who can interact comfortably with strangers and keep their cool in stressful situations. It's also important to be physically fit, as attendants are on their feet for most of the flight. A person's vision and height also comes into play because attendants frequently have to reach into overhead bins and serve passengers hot liquids. Some airlines even require 20/30 vision or better with glasses.

Nowadays, most airlines will allow you to submit your résumé online, which greatly simplifies the process of applying for a position. With the exception of the interview, almost every part of the application process can be accomplished online. The interview is a crucial part of the process, so preparation is essential. Not only will your personality and customer service experience be assessed, but your appearance and spoken manner is also important.

Secrets for Success

See the following suggestions and turn to the appendix for advice on résumés and interviews.

✴ Never lose your patience! Being a flight attendant is both physically and mentally exhausting, but a good flight attendant will never let his or her exhaustion show. A sunny disposition is a secret to success in this business.

✴ Pay close attention to those around you. Things can turn from routine to urgent in very little time. Also keep a good rapport with your colleagues so that you work well together when things get stressful.

Reality Check

If flight attendants are not mindful, injuries can occur when opening overhead compartments or while pushing heavy service carts. In addition, flight attendants occasionally develop stress disorders from working long hours in a pressurized environment.

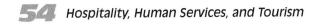

Some Other Jobs to Think About

✯ Reservation ticket agent. Ticket agents also work for airlines and deal with nervous flyers. As a result, they receive customer service training similar to that of flight attendants.

✯ Public-relations specialist. This job also requires you to have strong communication skills as well as a pulled-together appearance.

✯ EMT. Like flight attendants, emergency medical technicians are safety professionals whose job it is to be calm even under trying circumstances.

How You Can Move Up

✯ Like most jobs, putting in extra hours goes a long way in the airline industry. Most airlines guarantee a minimum of 65 to 85 flight hours per month, with the option to work additional hours. If you work hard and offer to work additional hours, not only will your superiors take notice but you'll also receive extra compensation for your time.

✯ After you have demonstrated that you are resourceful in crisis situations and capable of handling the job, you could be promoted to lead attendant, the highest attendant position aboard the aircraft. Lead attendants manage the other attendants aboard the aircraft and often take on additional responsibilities, such as recruiting and instructing other attendants.

✯ After working as a lead attendant, if you decide to move into another field, the experiences you've gathered as a flight attendant will prepare you for a host of other airline and non–airline-related jobs. Many flight attendants have gone on to become human resource managers, travel agents, public relations professionals, and airline consultants.

Web Sites to Surf

Association of Flight Attendants. The majority of flight attendants belong to this union. Their Web site teaches you a lot about what it means to be a flight attendant. http://www.afanet.org

Thirty Thousand Feet. This is a Web site specifically geared toward helping you find jobs in the airline industry. It's an informative site that can link you to some great job openings. http://www.thirtythousandfeet.com/flightat.htm

Airline Career. This is another great Web site. Once you become a member, you can enroll in their flight attendant training program. http://airlinecareer.com

Make guests' stays memorable

Hotel Desk Clerk, Concierge, or Reservation Agent

Meet interesting and diverse people

Be the face of your employer

Hotel Desk Clerk, Concierge, or Reservation Agent

Eloise, the infamous children's book character who grew up at the Plaza Hotel, once said of hotel life that "getting bored is not allowed." Anyone who has ever worked at a hotel would probably agree with Eloise. When you're a desk clerk, concierge, or reservation agent, there's seldom a dull moment on the job. Your days are spent greeting guests and working out the details of their reservations, fulfilling their particular needs and desires, and advising them on where to go and what to see.

Hotels—which include resorts, extended-stay residences, and casinos—are located in every major town and city, and in far-flung spots of scenic beauty, which means that you could find work almost anywhere. Although high-end and high-volume establishments employ the greatest number of people, many smaller hotels and motels hire desk clerks with little or no experience in the field. So if your organization is good and you enjoy meeting and serving people, this may be the job for you.

Is This Job For You?

To find out if working in hotel is right for you, read each of the following questions and answer "Yes" or "No."

Yes	*No*	**1.**	Are you highly personable?
Yes	*No*	**2.**	Can you think on your feet and handle crisis situations?
Yes	*No*	**3.**	Do you have strong computer skills?
Yes	*No*	**4.**	Are you willing to work late nights and weekends?
Yes	*No*	**5.**	Are you good at answering phones and talking with customers?
Yes	*No*	**6.**	Could you work in a fast-paced environment?
Yes	*No*	**7.**	Do you speak English fluently?
Yes	*No*	**8.**	Do you dress in a neat and professional fashion?
Yes	*No*	**9.**	Are you patient and understanding?
Yes	*No*	**10.**	Do you think you would enjoy working in a hotel environment?

If you answered "Yes" to most of the questions, working in the front operations of a hotel may be right for you. To find out more, read on.

Let's Talk Money

Hotel desk clerks earn a median annual income of $19,480, according to 2006 figures from the U.S. Bureau of Labor Statistics; concierges and reservation agents, who tend to receive higher salaries, both earn an average of about $25,000 per year.

What You'll Do

Front desk clerks greet guests from all over the world, assign them rooms, and close out their accounts at the end of their stays. Though this may seem easy enough, imagine what it's like when a guest is not ready to leave at "checkout," and you have other people waiting for the room. Or imagine when you have to settle a dispute about room charges. In addition to these sorts of guest duties, data recording is important to hotel marketing and overall service, so it is a desk clerk's job to keep records of room assignments and other registration-related information on computers.

At large hotels and resorts, the staff assignments are fairly complex. In addition to having several desk clerks and a front desk manager, large hotels and resorts typically have a concierge. Concierges and desk clerks are the most visible hotel employees, which is the reason their appearance and general manner must be impeccable.

The word concierge derives from the French term *comtes des cierges,* meaning "keeper of the candles." In modern terms, a concierge guides and advises the guests. It is the concierge who provides guests with inside information and tells them where to find the best sites, souvenirs, restaurants, and attractions. Concierges must have the patience of a saint and the people skills of a politician. Good concierges don't just know the best restaurants in town, they also know the people who run them. It's not uncommon for guests to approach the concierge and say, "We need a reservation for three and a cab right now." Concierges are usually the ones who deal with demanding or high-profile guests, which can be stressful at times. They (along with front desk clerks) also keep track of the needs and wants of guests, so return visitors will have their rooms set at just the temperature they prefer and receive their wake-up calls at the right time, without having to request it.

Although reservation agents work in offices where they're not on display, their jobs can be equally stressful. It is their responsibility to book rooms, quote rates, and answer any travel or scheduling questions that a guest may have. They spend a lot of time either talking to customers on the phone or answering e-mail inquiries about routes, schedules, rates, and types of accommodation. The job requires them to be proficient on the computer because reservation agents use proprietary networks to obtain information needed to make, change, or cancel reservations for customers.

In each of these positions—concierge, desk clerk, or reservation agent—work at times may feel like being in the midst of a traveling circus. However, beyond the day-to-day tasks, working in a hotel can be a fascinating experience. To fully appreciate the job, however, an employee must be willing to listen to and accommodate a diverse group of individuals, each with particular desires, attitudes, and even customs.

Who You'll Work For

- ✳ Commercial hotels
- ✳ Residential and extended-stay hotels
- ✳ Bed-and-breakfasts
- ✳ Inns
- ✳ Motels
- ✳ Resorts
- ✳ Casino hotels

Let's Talk Trends

The hotel business is on an upswing. According to 2006 figures from the Bureau of Labor Statistics, about 214,000 people work as hotel desk clerks or concierges, an increase of 5 percent over the prior biennium. In addition, hotels have a great track record when it comes to hiring young people with little or no customer-service experience. According to the bureau, about 19 percent of hotel workers are younger than 25, compared with about 14 percent across all other industries.

Where You'll Work

Most concierges and hotel reservation agents work for large chains because they have the highest volume of guests and reservations. Though the environment in a large hotel may not be as relaxed as at a smaller, family-run establishment, corporate-owned hotels and chains offer perks, such as discounts on travel rates, better benefits, and larger bonuses. Some corporate chains even help their employees further their education by assisting with the cost of hotel management coursework.

Although corporate hotels and chains technically employ more people, smaller hotels and motels with 10 or fewer employees still outnumber large ones. In these sorts of establishments, clerks often assume the responsibilities of both the concierge and the front desk manager. In addition to registering guests and answering the phones, clerks also bring fresh linens to rooms, handle the bookkeeping, and advise guests on places to visit. Although the responsibilities can be daunting at times, desk clerks have more autonomy at smaller establishments and may develop a better rapport with guests. Every type of establishment, however, has its share of demanding guests and stressful situations. For this reason, it's important for employees at these establishments to be levelheaded and patient.

Your Typical Day

Here are the highlights of a front desk clerk's day.

✓ **Arrive before the guests wake up.** You usually arrive by 5 a.m. to check that wake-up calls and room-service orders are in place. Occasionally, you'll receive a call saying that a lightbulb went out in room 105 or that room 256 needs some aspirin, but usually the early mornings are the quietest time. You start going over the room assignments for the day.

✓ **Check them out.** New guests typically start arriving after noon, which means that you need to have guests checked out and start the cleaning of the rooms well beforehand. If a guest hasn't checked out by 11:30, you give the room a call. In the midst of checking out, you'll also have to deal with your manager informing you of last-minute changes and requests.

✓ **Check them in.** You review your registration list before everyone starts arriving. You see that Ms. Wiles, a favored guest, is

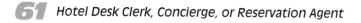

The Inside Scoop: Q&A

Zoe Merrill
Front desk clerk
Los Angeles, California

Q: *How did you get your job?*

A: I applied for the job on Monster.com and received a response immediately. Several days later,
I went in for an interview. The management was very laid-back,
and the general feel of the place really appealed to me. I guess they
thought I was a good fit for them as well because I was hired on
the spot.

Q: *What do you like best about your job?*

A: As a child, I played secretary a lot, so—not surprisingly—I like
filing, answering the phones, and problem solving. While I don't
mind working in a people-oriented environment, the best part for
me is being organized and handling administrative tasks.

Q: *What's the most challenging part of your job?*

A: Trying to please everyone is definitely the most challenging part
of the job. You have to keep both the management and the guests
happy, which can be difficult, particularly if you're dealing with a
demanding guest.

Q: *What are the keys to success to being a front desk clerk?*

A: To be successful as a front desk agent you need to have patience.
If you're organized and able to multitask, that will certainly help,
but good communication is what matters most. If you're able to
articulate your thoughts in a clear and eloquent fashion, you will
go a long way in this business.

checking in and make a note to address her by name. As
guests arrive, you greet them warmly, and if you can tell from
the reservation agent's notes that a guest just flew in, ask them
how their flight was. Most important, you get their credit card
number and give them their room key and other pertinent information to help them get oriented and settled in their room.

What You Can Do Now

✯ Take classes in high school, such as speech, English, computers, and business that will give you an edge when working with customers or managing your other responsibilities.

✯ Decide what sort of lodging establishment would best suit your personality. For example, could you picture yourself in a glitzy casino hotel? Or a quaint bed-and-breakfast?

✯ Check out the lodging management program that the Educational Institute of the American Hotel and Lodging Association (AHLA) offers to high school students.

✯ Research the lodging establishments in your area, and find out if any of the ones that interest you are looking for part-time employees.

What Training You'll Need

Experience carries almost as much weight as formal training in the hotel industry. Many hotels have a two-day orientation period, and if you are working as a front desk clerk or reservation agent, you don't need much more than that to get by. At an orientation, you will be introduced to your fellow employees and then given a detailed tour of every aspect of the hotel, from the emergency exits to the ice machine room. Hotel policies and regulations will also be explained during orientation. Many hotels and motels also have on-the-job training to supplement the orientation period. It is during this training period that desk clerks and reservation agents are taught how to use the computerized reservation and billing systems.

If you are seriously committed to working in the hotel industry, you might want to consider formal training. Upper management positions, such as general manager, hotel manager, food service manager, or sales manager typically require academic training in addition to on-the-job experience. Even if you don't desire a career as a manager, enrolling in a hotel management program or taking a class in this area is a good idea to keep in mind for the future. There are more than 800 schools across the United States that offer associate's degrees in hotel and restaurant management. Most of these programs provide students with both academic training and work experience in the various departments of a hotel.

For young go-getters who want to take hospitality courses while still in high school, the Educational Institute of the American Hotel and Lodging Association (AHLA) has initiated lodging management programs in more than 450 high schools in the United States. Their two-year program for juniors and seniors teaches management principles and leads to a professional certification

If you do not have the time or the money for formal training, work on your customer service skills on your own. Although businesses would prefer employees to be experienced from day one, in the long run, computer skills and fire drills are easier to teach than personal relations. What matters most is that a desk clerk, reservation agent, or concierge is professional, likable, and uses good judgment. The rest can be taught.

How to Talk Like A Pro

Here are a few words that you're likely to hear on the job:

* **Card entry** In lieu of a key, almost all hotels now use a card system to unlock hotel rooms. The entry card, which is about the size of a credit card, is set to work for however long a guest has paid to stay in the hotel.
* **Honesty bar** This is hotel-speak for an unattended beverage bar in the lobby or lounge of a hotel, where payment is left to the patron. By contrast, anything taken from a room minibar is automatically charged to the guest's account.
* **HVAC** This acronym, which stands for "heating, ventilation, and air conditioning," is frequently used to describe the hotel's climate control system.

How to Find a Job

Many small or independently run hotels hire high school workers as part-time desk clerks, so if you are willing to work at night or during holiday periods, a front office job can serve as a great stepping-stone to a full-time job. The best way to land an entry-level hotel job—be it a full or part time position—is to find a hotel or motel that interests you, introduce yourself to the manager, and ask him or her if there are any job openings available. This sort of friendly and direct approach is just what hotel managers are looking for in an employee. Remember, though, to dress as professionally as the job would require.

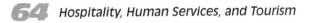

Secrets for *Success*

See the following suggestions and turn to the appendix for advice on résumés and interviews:

✦ Project your best self. Apart from having a winning personality, being detail-oriented can really make a difference. Skills like good spelling and a clear speaking voice can really make a difference.

✦ *Parlez-vous francais?* Because many hotels attract an international clientele, speaking a foreign language can be very helpful, particularly at high-end hotels and resorts.

Reality Check

Automated check-in and checkout procedures reduce the backlog of guests waiting for desk service and may reduce peak front-desk staffing needs in many establishments. Nevertheless, the front desk remains the principal point of contact for guests at most properties. Backlogs at busy checkout times can happen quickly and guests needing to make flights can get quite irate.

Some Other Jobs to Think About

✦ Real estate agent. As with the work of reservation agents, this job entails a lot of social talking with clients and prospective customers—here, to sell or rent an apartment or house.

✦ Restaurant host or hostess. Restaurants and hotels can have the same frenetic pace and energy. To work in either, employees must have patience and stamina. In addition, they need impeccable customer service skills.

How You Can Move Up

✦ Just as many Hollywood executives began their careers in studio mailrooms, many hotel owners started as bellhops and worked their way up. Front office jobs at hotels can serve as a great stepping-stone to management positions.

⭐ After a few years of working the desk, clerks are typically rewarded with promotions. Though it is often easier to find work at a small inn or motel, large hotel and motel chains have greater advancement opportunities.

⭐ Chain hotels and motels also typically have programs designed to help employees set and achieve career goals. Large hotels and chains also have management training programs, in which desk clerks and concierges are sometimes asked to participate.

Web Sites to Surf

American Hotel and Lodging Association. This professional association is a leading organization in the hospitality field and provides much useful information on its Web site for people interested in learning more about a career as a lodging professional. http://www.ahla.com

HCareers. This is a jobs board and research site presented by the hospitality industry and includes many useful links for people wanting to learn more about the scope of opportunities. http://www.hcareers.com

Make the calls that count

Baseball Umpire

Be in the midst of the action

Watch the games up close

Baseball Umpire

Behind every great baseball player, there's always an umpire. Truly. Umpires stand behind the bases, and although they might not hit the winning run, they're always the ones to call it. The fate and integrity of every baseball game rests on the umpire's shoulders, which is why some of the more notable "umps" have been inducted into the Baseball Hall of Fame. Success at this level requires good judgment, thick skin, and a love of the game.

At times, being an umpire can be a thankless job, but if you can look beyond the boos and the occasional peanut throw, there's nothing quite like seeing a home run from behind home plate. It's a demanding job, both mentally and physically, but If you enjoy sports and like to call all the shots, you could be one of the lucky few who do it for a living.

Is This Job For You?

To find out if being a professional umpire is the right job for you, read each of the following questions and answer "Yes" or "No."

Yes No	**1.**	Are you a serious baseball fan?
Yes No	**2.**	Did you grow up playing or watching sports?
Yes No	**3.**	Are you highly exact and detail-oriented?
Yes No	**4.**	Can you handle stressful situations?
Yes No	**5.**	Do you like making judgment calls?
Yes No	**6.**	Would your friends call you extremely fair-minded and morally sound?
Yes No	**7.**	Do you have 20/20 vision with or without corrective lenses?
Yes No	**8.**	Do you have good communication skills?
Yes No	**9.**	Are you a team player?
Yes No	**10.**	Would you like to travel for work?

If you answered "Yes" to most of the questions, you may have what it takes to be an umpire. To find out more about this profession, read on.

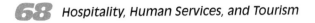

Let's Talk Money

According to 2006 data from the U.S. Bureau of Labor Statistics, the median annual earnings umpires is $44,866. However, major league salaries start at about $120,000.

What You'll Do

We all know that umpires call all the shots, but we often forget just how much pressure and responsibility come with that. Every foul, run, hit, or strike that is made this year will be called by one of the major league's 68 umpires, and unlike referees in American football, the umpire's judgment call is final. The job carries a lot of responsibility, and with it a lot of temptation, which is why umpires must be levelheaded.

As a professional umpire, your primary job is to encourage sportsmanship and to promote fair and safe play. Though this may seem like simply a matter of strong morals and a positive attitude, in fact it takes a tremendous level of skill and experience to be able to call a play. First you need to know how to position yourself according to the play. You should know approximately where a ball is going to land before the hitter even connects with the ball.

The home plate umpire is generally said to have the hardest job, which is the reason he or she is given the title umpire-in-chief. It's not uncommon for the plate ump to make over 300 calls in one night—and to be able to do that with accuracy, you need to have a lot of experience and training. Most umpires come into the majors after having worked from 8 to 12 years in the minor leagues.

Like athletes and coaches, umpires chose this profession because they have a love for the game. However, a thorough knowledge of the rule book is what matters most on the field. You may think you know baseball, but there are countless rules that even avid sports fans might not be aware of. Take this scenario: There's a player on first who's running on a pitch. The catcher throws the ball to second, but mid-throw his elbow hits the umpire's mask. The ball sails into centerfield, and the runner starts heading for third, but just as he reaches the base the centerfielder tags him.

While most would say that the runner is out, according to the Major League Baseball rule book, he gets to return to first because only a catcher's throw can retire a runner. Umpires must be able to make a technical call like this within seconds of the play. It's a job that requires a surprising amount of brainpower.

In addition to the mental workout, umpires also need to be in good physical shape. Depending on where an umpire is positioned, he or she is either squatting to call a pitch, ducking to miss a fly ball, or hustling to see a play. With all this action, it's important to stay in shape, particularly now that the leagues require umpires to pass an annual physical that includes a stress treadmill test and a squat test, as well an eye and orthopedic examination and a concussion baseline test.

One element of the umpire's life that most people associate with the players is the element of camaraderie. Few people realize that umpires have their own sense of team spirit. Umpires in both the minors and the majors work in crews. In the major leagues, there are 17 closely-knit crews of four. During away games, these crews often travel and eat together.

There is a very low turnover rate for umpires in the major leagues, so everyone really gets a chance to know each other. By contrast, there are more umpires in the minor leagues and the turnover rate is much higher, so it can be harder to create meaningful bonds. There's also a lot of competition in the minors as every umpire is vying for the same spot in the majors, but if you're good at what you do, you'll rise in the ranks with other talented umpires and make friends along the way.

Umpires stick together in part because they share a passion for the game but also because being an umpire can sometimes be isolating and exhausting. In addition to all the traveling, umpires often have to contend with disgruntled fans, players, and coaches. Sports games have the ability to bring out some pretty heated emotions in even the most passive people. During intense games or when two rival teams are playing, coaches and players have been known to verbally and even physically abuse umpires just because they didn't agree with a call.

Who You'll Work For

⚹ Little League teams
⚹ Minor League Baseball
⚹ Major League Baseball

Let's Talk Trends

Umpires and referees held 13,790 jobs in 2006. Altogether there are only 68 umpires in the major leagues, and 225 in the minors. Many professional umpires make good money working for colleges and universities. In addition, there are thousands of umpires who work part-time.

Where You'll Work

An umpire's office is home plate. Schools and Little Leagues, Major and Minor League Baseball all have need of umpires. Whether the backstop is in a community park or Yankee Stadium, the umpire will have traveled to get there, even if from just across town. Usually the umpire will change into game gear in a locker room at the stadium. When the competition ends, the umpire hits the showers and heads for a meal and some downtime (an umpire needs a healthful regimen to stay fresh for the season). Although the work takes place outside, it is usually under conditions that are comfortable for a person in a short-sleeved shirt or a light sweater. Sunblock, though, should find a place in the umpire's toiletries bag, given all time spent working in exposed areas and traveling. In the off-season, an umpire may pursue professional development through a program that would typically be offered at an educational campus. Most would also have to give spend a little office time to track invoices and cultivate future work.

Your Typical Day

Here are the highlights of a typical day as a major league umpire.

- ✓ **Prepare with ritual.** You're playing Arizona, and it's an away game. Like athletes, umpires keep a very strict schedule and are often prone to superstitions. You arrive at the stadium at your usual time—exactly two hours before game time—and after sharing a laugh with the crew and putting on your lucky pair of socks, everyone goes over the assignments.
- ✓ **Work the plate.** You're the home-plate umpire, so even before the anthem, your head is in the game. Everything is running smoothly and you're making quick and decisive calls, but at the bottom of the eighth inning things get ugly. Arizona is behind by one, and you call a controversial strike that results in the end of the inning. The Arizona manager goes ballistic and throws a

The Inside Scoop: Q&A

Jim Evans
Former Major League Baseball umpire
(28 years) and umpiring school owner
Kissimmee, Florida

Q: *How did you get started?*

A: Like most umpires, I started as a player when
I was 14 years old. My league at the time hosted a tournament
of out-of-town teams, and they needed umpires. Since I was a
catcher, the league's umpire-in-chief thought I would make a good
plate umpire. My first day, I worked five games, and I enjoyed the
experience so much that soon after I began umpiring on the days
that I wasn't playing. Before long I was enjoying the umpiring
more than the playing. I paid my way through college umpiring
youth leagues, high school, and college ball. Upon graduation, I
decided to give professional umpiring a try, so I went to umpire
school and graduated at the top of my class. From there, I went
on to enjoy a 32-year career in professional baseball, 28 in the
major leagues.

Q: *What do you like best about your job?*

A: The spontaneity. When you walk onto the field for a game, you
have no idea what's in store. I have worked the longest game in
major league history (8 hours and 7 minutes), and I have worked
no-hitters. I once worked three years without having to eject a
player, and then I've had to eject five in one game. Tough situations and rough weather conditions also keep the job interesting.
I've worked April games in the snow, and I've worked games in
125-degree weather. There is no script in baseball. Every game is
a new and different melodrama.

Q: *What's the most challenging part of your job?*

A: The most challenging part of the job is staying motivated during
the lulls and slow spots of a baseball game. If you do not talk to
yourself and stay prepared, you are likely to make a mistake.
Also, for professional umpires, being on the road a lot can make it
difficult to concentrate.

(continued on next page)

(continued from previous page)

Q: *What are the keys to success to being an umpire?*

A: The first key is understanding your responsibilities. Knowing your specific duties and how they are divided among you and your crew is paramount. The second key is recognizing play possibilities. Once the ball is pitched, a multitude of things can happen. Reacting to the appropriate cues will enable you to acquire the proper position and make the correct call. Lastly, success is developing the proper mindset. Though you may not have a multimillion-dollar contract like some of the players, you should be just as proud of what you do. Without umpires there could be no game.

bucket of water in your direction. Following a consultation between the umpires, the manager is ejected from the game.

✓ **Wrap up post-game.** After squatting behind the plate for 285 pitches, your team wins. Before returning to the umpire locker room to review the game, you should report the ejection to the league president, who is in charge of doling out penalties. If your back or knees hurt from squatting, you opt for a treatment from one of the sports physicians. Otherwise, you shower in the locker room and head back to the hotel to rest before getting up and doing it all over again.

What You Can Do Now

✴ Study the umpire rule book, work out regularly, and watch as many games as possible.

✴ Get in touch with a minor or major league umpire in your area, so you can gain personal insight into what an umpire's life is like. Volunteer with the umps if you can.

✴ Contact a little league association, and volunteer to be an umpire for a local league.

What Training You'll Need

To break into the clubby world of professional umpires it takes a lot of hard work, discipline, and training. Academically speaking, a high school diploma is all that's required of you, but if you want to work in the majors, you must attend one of the two training schools accredited by the Professional Baseball Umpire Corp. (PBUC).

The Jim Evans Academy in Kissimmee, Florida, and the Harry Wendelstedt School in Ormond Beach, Florida, are the gold standards in the industry. Both offer a highly competitive, five-week training course during baseball's off-season.

Together, the two schools graduate 400 to 500 students a year, but only 25 students from each school are recommended to the PBUC, which is in charge of selecting and overseeing minor league umpires. The 50 students then travel to the PBUC evaluation camp in March in Cocoa Beach, Florida, and those who perform the best are offered a job in the minors.

During training, you'll learn everything from hand signaling to the philosophy of umpiring. In addition to classroom work, there is a heavy physical component to most training programs. You'll receive instruction on the two-person umpiring system, and be asked to perform intense two-person drills. You'll also do a lot of plate work in the batting cage, but the most challenging aspect is the simulation of real games, also known as trial by fire. During these sessions student umpires face unusual situations, where they are forced to make calls and defend them against complaints from instructors pretending to be coaches, managers, and players. This method of instruction is meant to steel the nerves and strengthen the student's resolve. It's an important component of the training because managers keep track of the umpires and when they see a new ump on the field, they often test their limits.

Other training includes angle-and-distance drills and pitch-calling drills, in which mirrors, measuring sticks, and video cameras are often employed for accuracy.

Finally, let's not forget your own physical training. While the athletes may be the ones sprinting for the ball or rounding the bases, the umpire is never too far behind. In order to have success on the field, you need to work out daily, and live a healthy lifestyle.

How to Talk Like A Pro

Here are some words that you're likely to hear as a professional umpire:

- ✴ **Adjudged** This is the official word for an umpire's decision.
- ✴ **Blues** Referees are sometimes referred to as blues because their uniforms are often blue in color.

✦ **Dead ball** This is a ball that is out of play because of a legally created temporary suspension of play.

✦ **Overslide** When an offensive player slides to a base with such momentum that he loses contact with the base.

How to Find a Job

Although competition is stiff in the umpiring field, there are plenty of part-time jobs available for beginners looking to gain experience—though typically for very little or no pay. If you're still in high school, the Little Leagues are a great place to volunteer. And if you contact your regional Little League headquarters and sign up for a two- or four-day umpire clinic, you'll be on the field in no time. For high school athletics, you'll need to register with a state agency and pass an exam on the rules of the game before you can start umpiring. Contact the National Federation of State High School Associations (NFHS, http://www.nfhs.org) for information on openings in your area.

Once you've gained enough experience in the field, you can start thinking about college umpiring. This can be a competitive environment, but unlike the little leagues or high school athletics, you are paid a decent salary. College umpires must be certified by an official training school and be evaluated during a probationary period. If you do well at the college level, you will be admitted into the minors, where both the talent and the pay are greater.

The minor leagues are divided into four levels: rookie, short-season, long-season and advanced "A." Depending on your competency, you will start in the rookie or short-season league, and rise through the ranks until you make it to the majors. Although there are a lot of people vying for a small number of positions, professional umpires have a very high retention rate, so if you work hard and make it into the professional leagues, you're set for life.

Secrets for Success

See the following suggestions and turn to the appendix for advice on résumés and interviews.

✦ Calling all the shots doesn't make you a hot shot. As an umpire, you have a surprising amount of authority and power on the field, which is the reason it's important to keep your ego in check. The best umpires are humble, accurate, and unbiased.

✳ Always keep your eye on the ball while it's in play. It is more important to know just where a fly ball fell, or a thrown ball finished up, than whether a runner missed a base.

Reality Check

Nowadays, with the advent of technologies like instant replay and slow-motion cameras, an umpire's accuracy rate needs to be near perfect. In order to make it to the big leagues, almost all of your calls must be on the money. According to Major League Baseball, its umpires have a 97 percent accuracy rate for balls and strikes. If your accurate rate isn't in the same ballpark, the chances of making it to the big leagues are slim.

Some Other Jobs to Think About

✳ Coach. This is a sports job that requires you to be a confident decision maker. However, unlike umpires, coaches devise strategies instead of making calls. They also form intense bonds with the players on their team, and often have rivalries with other coaches in their league.

✳ Fitness instructor. With this profession, there is an emphasis on being physically fit and active, and as with umpiring, the job requires a lot of energy, enthusiasm, and leadership skills.

How You Can Move Up

✳ Unlike minor league ballplayers, who are often recruited by the majors after only two seasons, umpires typically work in the minors for seven to ten years before they can be considered for the majors. To move up, you've got to be physically fit, work well with others, and have a high accuracy rate. Punctuality and appearance are also taken very seriously in this profession. In umpire school, being early, rather than on time, is stressed, and everyone receives instruction on how to clean a uniform. One umpire named Bill McGowan was inducted into the Baseball Hall of Fame for having gone 16 years without missing one inning. McGowan umpired 2,541 consecutive games; if you can do even half as many, you're guaranteed to move up in the ranks.

✴ Just as good players today now rely on video programming to study opposing pitchers and hitters, the best umpires frequently review game calls. The more you know about the game, the better your chances are of succeeding, so hit the rule books and study every game.

Web Sites to Surf

The World Umpires Association. This site provides you with a bevy of insider information on the umpire lifestyle. It includes blogs, statistics, and news updates on umpires. It also gives you tips on how to become an umpire. http://www.worldumpires.com/index.php?option

Jim Evans Academy of Professional Training. Jim Evans is one of the two accredited umpire training schools that you'll need to attend if you plan on becoming a professional umpire. The site explains their program philosophy and guides you through the application process. http://www.umpireacademy.com

Minor League Baseball. This site offers great information on umpiring in the major and minor leagues. It also has a lot of information on the PBUC. http://web.minorleaguebaseball.com/index.jsp

Unlock your network

Appendix A

Get your résumé ready

Ace your interview

Putting Your Best Foot Forward

When 20-year-old Justin Schulman started job-hunting for a position as a fitness trainer—the first step toward managing a fitness facility—he didn't mess around. "I immediately opened the Yellow Pages and started calling every number listed under health and fitness, inquiring about available positions," he recalls. Schulman's energy and enterprise paid off: He wound up with interviews that led to several offers of part-time work.

Schulman's experience highlights an essential lesson for job seekers: There are plenty of opportunities out there, but jobs won't come to you—especially the career-oriented, well-paying ones that that you'll want to stick with over time. You've got to seek them out.

Uncover Your Interests

Whether you're in high school or bringing home a full-time paycheck, the first step toward landing your ideal job is assessing your interests. You need to figure out what makes you tick. After all, there is a far greater chance that you'll enjoy and succeed in a career that taps into your passions, inclinations, and natural abilities. That's what happened with career-changer Scott Rolfe. He was already 26 when he realized he no longer wanted to work in the food industry. "I'm an avid outdoorsman," Rolfe says, "and I have an appreciation for natural resources that many people take for granted." Rolfe turned his passions into his ideal job as a forestry technician.

If you have a general idea of what your interests are, you're far ahead of the game. You may know that you're cut out for a health care career, for instance, or one in business. You can use a specific volume of Great Careers with a High School Diploma to discover what position to target. If you are unsure of your direction, check out the whole range of volumes to see the scope of jobs available.

You can also use interest inventories and skills-assessment programs to further pinpoint your ideal career. Your school or public librarian or guidance counselor should be able to help you locate such assessments. Web sites, such as America's Career InfoNet (http://www.acinet.org) and Jobweb.com, also offer interest inventories.

You'll find suggestions for Web sites related to specific careers at the end of each chapter in any Great Careers with a High School Diploma volume.

Unlock Your Network

The next stop toward landing the perfect job is networking. The word may make you cringe, but networking is simply introducing yourself and exchanging job-related and other information that may prove helpful to one or both of you. That's what Susan Tinker-Muller did. Quite a few years ago, she struck up a conversation with a fellow passenger on her commuter train. Little did she know that the natural interest she expressed in the woman's accounts payable department would lead to news about a job opening there. Tinker-Muller's networking landed her an entry-level position in accounts payable with MTV Networks. She is now the accounts payable administrator.

Tinker-Muller's experience illustrates why networking is so important. Fully 80 percent of openings are *never* advertised, and more than half of all employees land their jobs through networking, according to the U.S. Bureau of Labor Statistics. That's 8 out of 10 jobs that you'll miss if you don't get out there and talk with people. And don't think you can bypass face-to-face conversations by posting your résumé on job sites like Craigslist.org, Monster.com, and Hotjobs.com and then waiting for employers to contact you. That's so mid-1990s! Back then, tens of thousands, if not millions, of job seekers diligently posted their résumés on scores of sites. Then they sat back and waited . . . and waited . . . and waited. You get the idea. Big job sites have their place, of course, but relying solely on an Internet job search is about as effective throwing your résumé into a black hole.

Begin your networking efforts by making a list of people to talk to: teachers, classmates (and their parents), anyone you've worked with, neighbors, members of your church, synogogue, temple or mosque, and anyone you've interned or volunteered with. You can also expand your networking opportunities through the student sections of industry associations; attending or volunteering at industry events, association conferences, career fairs; and through job-shadowing. Keep in mind that only rarely will any of the people on your list be in a position to offer you a job. But whether they know it or not, they probably know someone who knows someone who is. That's why your networking goal is not to ask for a job but the name of someone to talk with. Even when you network with an employer, it's wise to say something like, "You may not have any positions available, but would you know someone I could talk with to find out more about what it's like to work in this field?"

Also, keep in mind that networking is a two-way street. For instance, you may be talking with someone who has a job opening that isn't appropriate for you. If you can refer someone else to the employer, either person may well be disposed to help you someday in the future.

Dial-Up Help

Call your contacts directly, rather than e-mail them. (E-mails are too easy for busy people to ignore, even if they don't mean to.) Explain that you're a recent graduate; that Mr. Jones referred you; and that you're wondering if you could stop by for 10 or 15 minutes at your contact's convenience to find out a little more about how the industry works. If you leave this message as a voicemail, note that you'll call back in a few days to follow up. If you reach your contact directly, expect that they'll say they're too busy at the moment to see you. Ask, "Would you mind if I check back in a couple of weeks?" Then jot down a note in your date book or set up a reminder in your computer calendar and call back when it's time. (Repeat this above scenario as needed, until you get a meeting.)

Once you have arranged to talk with someone in person, prep yourself. Scour industry publications for insightful articles; having up-to-date knowledge about industry trends shows your networking contacts that you're dedicated and focused. Then pull together questions about specific employers and suggestions that will set you apart from the job-hunting pack in your field. The more specific your questions (for instance, about one type of certification versus another), the more likely your contact will see you as an "insider," worthy of passing along to a potential employer. At the end of any networking meeting, ask for the name of someone else who might be able to help you further target your search.

Get a Lift

When you meet with a contact in person (as well as when you run into someone fleetingly), you need an "elevator speech." This is a summary of up to two minutes that introduces who you are, as well as your experience and goals. An elevator speech should be short enough to be delivered during an elevator ride with a potential employer from the ground level to a high floor. In it, it's helpful to show that 1) you know the business involved; 2) you know the company; 3) you're qualified (give your work and educational information); and 4) you're goal-oriented, dependable, and hardworking. You'll be surprised how much information you can include in two minutes. Practice this speech in front of a mirror until you have the key points down very well. It should sound natural though, and you should come across as friendly, confident, and assertive. Remember, good eye contact needs to be part of your presentation as well as your everyday approach when meeting prospective employers or leads.

Get Your Résumé Ready

In addition to your elevator speech, another essential job-hunting tool is your résumé. Basically, a résumé is a little snapshot of you in words, reduced to one 8½ x 11-inch sheet of paper (or, at most, two sheets). You need a résumé whether you're in high school, college, or the workforce, and whether you've never held a job or have had many.

At the top of your résumé should be your heading. This is your name, address, phone numbers, and your e-mail address, which can be a sticking point. E-mail addresses such as sillygirl@yahoo.com or drinkingbuddy@hotmail.com won't score you any points. In fact they're a turn-off. So if you dreamed up your address after a night on the town, maybe it's time to upgrade. (And while we're on the subject, these days, potential employers often check Myspace pages, personal blogs, and Web sites. What's posted there has been known to cost candidates job offers.)

The first section of your résumé is a concise Job Objective: "Entry-level agribusiness sales representative seeking a position with a leading dairy cooperative." These days, with word-processing software, it's easy and smart to adapt your job objective to the position for which you're applying. An alternative way to start a résumé, which some recruiters prefer, is to rework the Job Objective into a Professional Summary. A Professional Summary doesn't mention the position you're seeking, but instead focuses on your job strengths: e.g., "Entry-level agribusiness sales rep; strengths include background in feed, fertilizer, and related markets and ability to contribute as a member of a sales team." Which is better? It's your call.

The body of a résumé typically starts with your Job Experience. This is a chronological list of the positions you've held (particularly the ones that will help you land the job you want). Remember: Never, never fudge anything. It is okay, however, to include volunteer positions and internships on the chronological list, as long as they're noted for what they are.

Next comes your Education section. Note: It's acceptable to flip the order of your Education and Job Experience sections if you're still in high school or don't have significant work experience. Summarize any courses you've taken in the job area you're targeting, any certifications you've achieved, relevant computer knowledge, special seminars, or other school-related experience that will distinguish you. Include your grade average if it's more than 3.0. Don't worry if you haven't finished your degree. Simply write that you're currently enrolled in your program (if you are).

In addition to these elements, other sections may include professional organizations you belong to and any work-related achievements, awards, or recognition you've received. Also, you can have a section for your interests, such as playing piano or soccer (and include any notable achievements regarding your interests, for instance, placed third in Midwest Regional Piano Competition). You should also note other special abilities, such as "Fluent in French," or "Designed own Web site." These sorts of activities will reflect well on you whether or not they are job-related.

You can either include your references or simply note, "References Upon Request." Be sure to ask your references permission to use their name, and alert them to the fact that they may be contacted, before you include them on your résumé. For more information on résumé writing, check out Web sites such as http://www.resume.monster.com.

Craft **Your Cover Letter**

When you apply for a job either online or by mail, it's appropriate to include a cover letter. A cover letter lets you convey extra information about yourself than doesn't fit or isn't always appropriate in your résumé. For instance, in a cover letter, you can and should mention the name of anyone who referred you to the job. You can go into some detail about the reason you're a great match, given the job description. You can also address any questions that might be raised in the potential employer's mind (for instance, a gap in your résumé). Don't, however, ramble on. Your cover letter should stay focused on your goal: To offer a strong, positive impression of yourself and persuade the hiring manager that you're worth an interview. Your cover letter gives you a chance to stand out from the other applicants and sell yourself. In fact, 23 percent of hiring managers say a candidate's ability to relate his or her experience to the job at hand is a top hiring consideration, according to a Careerbuilder.com survey.

You can write a positive, yet concise cover letter in three paragraphs: An introduction containing the specifics of the job you're applying for; a summary of why you're a good fit for the position and what you can do for the company; and a closing with a request for an interview, your contact information, and thanks. Remember to vary the structure and tone of your cover letter. For instance, don't begin every sentence with "I."

Ace Your Interview

Preparation is the key to acing any job interview. This starts with researching the company or organization you're interviewing with. Start with the firm, group, or agency's own Web site. Explore it thoroughly, read about their products and services, their history, and sales and marketing information. Check out their news releases, links that they provide, and read up on, or Google, members of the management team to get an idea of what they may be looking for in their employees.

Sites such as http://www.hoovers.com enable you to research companies across many industries. Trade publications in any industry (such as *Food Industry News*, *Hotel Business*, and *Hospitality Technology*) are also available at online or in hard copy at many college or public libraries. Don't forget to make a phone call to contacts you have in the organization to get a better idea of the company culture.

Preparation goes beyond research, however. It includes practicing answers to common interview questions:

- *Tell me about yourself.* Don't talk about your favorite bands or your personal history; give a brief summary of your background and interest in the particular job area.
- *Why do you want to work here?* Here's where your research into the company comes into play; talk about the firm's strengths and products or services.

✻ *Why should we hire you?* Now is your chance to sell yourself as a dependable, trustworthy, effective employee.

✻ *Why did you leave your last job?* Keep your answer short; never bad-mouth a previous employer. You can always say something simple, such as, "It wasn't a good fit, and I was ready for other opportunities."

Rehearse your answers, but don't try to memorize them. Responses that are natural and spontaneous come across better. Trying to memorize exactly what you want to say is likely to both trip you up and make you sound robotic.

As for the actual interview, to break the ice, offer a few pleasant remarks about the day, a photo in the interviewer's office, or something else similar. Then, once the interview gets going, listen closely and answer the questions you're asked, versus making any other point that you want to convey. If you're unsure whether your answer was adequate, simply ask, "Did that answer the question?" Show respect, good energy, and enthusiasm, and be upbeat. Employers are looking for workers who are enjoyable to be around, as well as good workers. Show that you have a positive attitude and can get along well with others by not bragging during the interview, overstating your experience, or giving the appearance of being too self-absorbed. Avoid one-word answers, but at the same time don't blather. If you're faced with a silence after giving your response, pause for a few seconds, and then ask, "Is there anything else you'd like me to add?" Never look at your watch and turn your cell phone off before an interview.

Near the interview's end, the interviewer is likely to ask you if you have any questions. Make sure that you have a few prepared, for instance:

✻ *"Tell me about the production process."*

✻ *"What's your biggest short-term challenge?"*

✻ *"How have recent business trends affected the company?"*

✻ *"Is there anything else that I can provide you with to help you make your decision?"*

✻ *"When will you make your hiring decision?"*

During a first interview, never ask questions like, "What's the pay?" "What are the benefits?" or "How much vacation time will I get?"

Find the Right Look

Appropriate dress and grooming is also essential to interviewing success. For business jobs and many other occupations, it's appropriate to come to an interview in a nice (not stuffy) suit. However, different fields have various dress codes. In the music business, for instance, "business casual" reigns for many jobs. This is a slightly modified look, where slacks and a jacket are just fine for a man, and a nice skirt and blouse and jacket or sweater are acceptable for a woman. Dressing overly "cool" will usually backfire.

In general, tend to all the basics from shoes (no sneakers, sandals, or overly high heels) to outfits (no short skirts for women). Women should also avoid attention-getting necklines. Keep jewelry to a minimum. Tattoos and body jewelry are becoming more acceptable, but if you can take out piercings (other than a simple stud in your ear), you're better off. Similarly, unusual hairstyles or colors may bias an employer against you, rightly or wrongly. Make sure your hair is neat and acceptable (consider getting a haircut). Also go light on the makeup, self-tanning products, body scents, and other grooming agents. Don't wear a baseball cap or any other type of hat, and by all means, take off your sunglasses!

Beyond your physical appearance, you already know to be well bathed to minimize odor (leave your home early if you tend to sweat, so you can cool off in private), use a breath mint (especially if you smoke) make good eye contact, smile, speak clearly using proper English (or Spanish), use good posture (don't slouch), offer a firm handshake, and arrive within five minutes of your interview. (If you're unsure of where you're going, Mapquest or Google Map it and consider making a dry run to the site so you won't be late.) First impressions can make or break your interview.

Remember to Follow Up

After your interview, send a thank-you note. This thoughtful gesture will separate you from most of the other candidates. It demonstrates your ability to follow through, and it catches your prospective employer's attention one more time. In a 2005 Careerbuilder.com survey, nearly 15 percent of 650 hiring managers said they wouldn't hire someone who failed to send a thank-you letter after the interview. Thirty-two percent say they would still consider the candidate, but would think less of him or her.

So do you hand write or e-mail the thank you letter? The fact is that format preferences vary. One in four hiring managers prefer to receive a thank-you note in e-mail form only; 19 percent want the e-mail, followed up with a hard copy; 21 percent want a typed hard-copy only, and 23 percent prefer just a handwritten note. (Try to check with an assistant on the format your potential employer prefers). Otherwise, sending an e-mail and a handwritten copy is a safe way to proceed.

Winning an Offer

There are no sweeter words to a job hunter than, "We'd like to hire you." So naturally, when you hear them, you may be tempted to jump at the offer. *Don't.* Once an employer wants you, he or she will usually give you some time to make your decision and get any questions you may have answered. Now is the time to get specific about salary, benefits, and negotiate some of these points. If you haven't already done so, check out salary ranges for your position and area of the country on sites such as Payscale.com, Salary.com, and Salaryexpert.com (basic info is free; specific requests are not). Also find out what sort of benefits similar jobs offer. Then don't be afraid to negotiate in a diplomatic way. Asking for better terms is reasonable and expected. You may worry that asking the employer to bump up his or her offer may jeopardize your job, but handled intelligently, negotiating for yourself may in fact be a way to impress your future employer and get a better deal for yourself.

After you've done all the hard work that successful job-hunting requires, you may be tempted to put your initiative into autodrive. However, the efforts you made to land your job—from clear communication to enthusiasm-are necessary now to pave your way to continued success. As Danielle Little, a human-resources assistant, says, "You must be enthusiastic and take the initiative. There is an urgency to prove yourself and show that you are capable of performing any and all related tasks. If your manager notices that you have potential, you will be given additional responsibilities, which will help advance your career." So do your best work on the job, and build your credibility. Your payoff will be career advancement and increased earnings.